DRUG ABUSE
INSIDE AN AMERICAN EPIDEMIC

By Nicole Horning

Portions of this book originally appeared in *Drug Abuse* by Hal Marcovitz.

LUCENT
PRESS

Published in 2019 by
Lucent Press, an Imprint of Greenhaven Publishing, LLC
353 3rd Avenue
Suite 255
New York, NY 10010

Designer: Seth Hughes
Editor: Jennifer Lombardo

Cataloging-in-Publication Data

Names: Horning, Nicole.
Title: Drug abuse: inside an American epidemic / Nicole Horning.
Description: New York : Lucent Press, 2019. | Series: Hot topics | Includes index.
Identifiers: ISBN 9781534563520 (pbk.) | ISBN 9781534563506 (library bound) | ISBN 9781534563513 (ebook)
Subjects: LCSH: Drug abuse–United States–Juvenile literature. |
  Drug abuse–Prevention–Juvenile literature. | Drug legalization–Juvenile literature. |
  Drug control–Juvenile literature.
Classification: LCC HV5801.H687 2019 | DDC 362.290973–dc23

Printed in the United States of America

CPSIA compliance information: Batch #BS18KL: For further information contact Greenhaven Publishing LLC, New York, New York at 1-844-317-7404.

Please visit our website, www.greenhavenpublishing.com. For a free color catalog of all our high-quality books, call toll free 1-844-317-7404 or fax 1-844-317-7405.

CONTENTS

Adolescence is a time when many people begin to take notice of the world around them. News channels, blogs, and talk radio shows are constantly promoting one view or another; very few are unbiased. Young people also hear conflicting information from parents, friends, teachers, and acquaintances. Often, they will hear only one side of an issue or be given flawed information. People who are trying to support a particular viewpoint may cite inaccurate facts and statistics on their blogs, and news programs present many conflicting views of important issues in our society. In a world where it seems everyone has a platform to share their thoughts, it can be difficult to find unbiased, accurate information about important issues.

It is not only facts that are important. In blog posts, in comments on online videos, and on talk shows, people will share opinions that are not necessarily true or false, but can still have a strong impact. For example, many young people struggle with their body image. Seeing or hearing negative comments about particular body types online can have a huge effect on the way someone views himself or herself and may lead to depression and anxiety. Although it is important not to keep information hidden from young people under the guise of protecting them, it is equally important to offer encouragement on issues that affect their mental health.

The titles in the Hot Topics series provide readers with different viewpoints on important issues in today's society. Many of these issues, such as teen pregnancy and Internet safety, are of immediate concern to young people. This series aims to give readers factual context on these crucial topics in a way that lets them form their own opinions. The facts presented throughout also serve to empower readers to help themselves or support people they know who are struggling with many of the challenges adolescents face today. Although negative viewpoints are not ignored or downplayed, this series allows young people to see that the challenges they face are not insurmountable. Eating disorders can be overcome, the Internet can be navigated safely, and pregnant teens do not have to feel hopeless.

Quotes encompassing all viewpoints are presented and cited so readers can trace them back to their original source, verifying for themselves whether the information comes from a reputable place. Additional books and websites are listed, giving readers a starting point from which to continue their own research. Chapter questions encourage discussion, allowing young people to hear and understand their classmates' points of view as they further solidify their own. Full-color photographs and enlightening charts provide a deeper understanding of the topics at hand. All of these features augment the informative text, helping young people understand the world they live in and formulate their own opinions concerning the best way they can improve it.

The Tragedy of Addiction

An alarming amount of money has been spent on drugs throughout American history. Since 1971, when President Richard Nixon declared a war on drugs, more than $1 trillion has been spent on fighting this war in America. Meanwhile, multiple drug cartels in places such as Mexico, Afghanistan, and Colombia are making millions of dollars off of people's drug addictions. In 2010, Americans spent $109 billion on the purchase of illegal drugs, up from $108 billion in 2000.

How to end drug abuse has become a topic of debate among many—from presidential candidates to law enforcement, and even the families of those who are suffering from an addiction or have tragically died. Some of these ideas target multiple factors. For instance, during the 2016 presidential election, Democratic candidate Hillary Clinton proposed a multi-faceted approach that was called the Initiative to Combat America's Deadly Epidemic of Drug and Alcohol Addiction. This initiative would have involved spending $10 billion on combating the drug epidemic, but it was clearly focused. The amount would have been spread out over the course of 10 years and "would be divided between a $7.5 billion fund to help states create programs tailored to the issues specific to their area and $2.5 billion allocated to the Substance Abuse Prevention and Treatment Block Grant, which directly funds substance-abuse treatment and prevention programs."[1] Also, part of the program would have been LifeSkills Training, which consisted of a three-year program that targeted substance abuse by middle-school students. Republican candidate Donald Trump proposed a wall to be built on the border between the United States and Mexico, which he stated was "'the source' of America's opioid problem."[2] However, while a majority of the drugs in the United States come by way of Mexico, it is not the only place they come from. Some criticized the idea of the wall, saying cartels would simply find another way to get their supplies in the hands of those who demand it—for instance, by building tunnels as they have before or using aircraft or boats.

While much of the drugs that come over the border are seized by Border Patrol agents, a good amount still makes it through, which means policy makers, schools, and more are getting just as creative at fighting the drug abuse epidemic. One way is through research-based prevention, which is a set of programs based on the most current scientific evidence that has been tested and shown to produce results. According to the National Institute on Drug Abuse (NIDA), "These prevention programs work to boost protective factors and eliminate or reduce risk factors for drug use. The programs are designed for various ages and can be designed for individual or group settings, such as the school and home."[3] The programs have three different options that are based on the students' risk factors.

Other programs that schools are developing are called collegiate recovery programs (CRP), which help students stay sober and stay in college. These programs include special on-campus housing, special activities, and counseling to help students become sober and stay that way, whether they have abused illegal drugs or alcohol.

For her 2016 presidential campaign, Hillary Clinton created a focused approach to combating drug addiction.

Donald Trump sees Mexico as the source of America's drug epidemic and proposed building a wall to end drug addiction.

While these programs are basic, there are more controversial ideas for treating drug abuse, and these include harm reduction and legalization of drugs. Harm reduction "aims to reduce the overall level of drug use among people who are unable or simply unwilling to stop. What should naturally follow is a decrease in the many negative consequences of drug use."[4] This program as well as the overall legalization of drugs both aim for the rehabilitation of the person rather than punishment. Some states have made a small step by legalizing marijuana, but as of early 2018, it is still illegal on the federal level.

The Impact on Loved Ones

Marijuana, heroin, and cocaine are three drugs talked about often in the media, but the topic of drug abuse is much broader than these drugs, which makes fighting them harder and the legal aspects more difficult. While heroin is at the center of a large epidemic that has taken many lives in recent years, a large part of this is due to the addition of fentanyl in the heroin powder. Fentanyl is a powerful painkiller that is about 50 times stronger than heroin; when added to heroin, it creates an even deadlier cocktail. However, fentanyl is not only found in illegal drugs such as heroin—it is also prescribed by doctors. Generally, when people hear the term "drug abuse," they may think of drugs such as heroin or cocaine, but prescription medications are also a large part of drug addiction. In particular, one class of prescription medication called opioids can lead to heroin addiction. This is because at a certain point, the amount of painkiller prescribed no longer does the job it is supposed to do. At this point, the person needs more and more, and heroin is often a stronger substitute. It is also cheaper and easier to get than prescription drugs. However, just as with the prescription medication, more and more heroin is needed to feel the same effect as the person eventually becomes used to the dose. At this point, they may experiment with other drugs or try rehabilitation. However, with rehabilitation comes the risk of relapse, which can be deadly because the person will generally not start with a small amount—out of habit, they will use the amount they were previously using. This often results in death because when they have not used heroin for some time, their body is no longer used to large doses.

Heroin is shown here. This drug has led to many overdoses and deaths.

While billions of dollars are spent on fighting the drug war, there is a much larger impact than just a financial one from either spending money on programs or housing an individual in prison. This issue largely affects the family and friends of the person who is addicted to drugs. It can create a lot of strain on families to see their loved one suffer through a painful and dangerous addiction, and it can cause heartbreak when the threat of death becomes a reality. Given the impact drug addiction has on society and loved ones, it is imperative to find how to best treat and end drug abuse.

CHAPTER 1

Drug Abuse in the United States

Drugs, whether for medicinal or recreational purposes, have a long history. Marijuana was mentioned in the Vedas, which are sacred Hindu texts, and it was also popularized during the Vietnam War. Opium comes from the opium poppy, which was referred to as a plant of joy by the Sumerians around 3400 BC. Opium was still used recreationally in the early 1800s by English literary figures such as poet John Keats. In the mid-1800s, morphine was created from opium, and it was found to be a powerful anesthetic that is still in use today for extreme pain. However, the creation of morphine also led to the creation of a much more powerful drug. There were originally good intentions for this new creation in 1895—a drug that did not have the common side effects of morphine and one that could be used as an ingredient in children's cough syrup. However, this drug, given the name "heroin" in 1895 and introduced commercially in 1898, turned out to be highly addictive—a fact that was discovered as early as 1899, according to *Business Insider* magazine, although it continued to be sold legally for several years despite these reports. In 1903, shortly after being introduced, heroin addiction was climbing. It was restricted and then outlawed, but even in 2018, the heroin epidemic continues. Since the early 1900s, waves of legislation have been passed and other drugs have been introduced, each carrying a risk of addiction—even when prescribed by a doctor.

Marijuana in Sacred Texts

Marijuana—the leaves of the cannabis plant—has been part of human culture for thousands of years. For instance, it was used by the Vikings and medieval Germans for things such as relieving pain from toothaches and childbirth. Its use was even recorded in the Vedas, a set of sacred Hindu texts, which were written around 2000 BC. These texts described marijuana as one of the five essential plants that brought happiness. There are also some reports that the ancient Greeks and Romans smoked and ate the plant. In 2016, archaeologists found cannabis in an ancient burial of a man who was about 35 years old in China. A total of "thirteen cannabis plants, each up to almost three feet long, were placed diagonally across the man's chest, with the roots oriented beneath his pelvis and the tops of the plants extending from just under his chin, up and alongside the left side of his face."[5] Radiocarbon dating placed the burial between 2,400 and 2,800 years ago. The heads of the plants that were found were covered in tiny plant hairs, called glandular trichomes. These secrete resin that contains psychoactive cannabinoids such as tetrahydrocannabinol (THC). This archaeological find leads researchers to believe cannabis may have been inhaled or consumed for medicinal or ritual purposes.

DECRIMINALIZATION: A PARTIAL SOLUTION

"The decriminalization of marijuana should be the first step toward a rational drug policy. The benefits would be felt immediately. Law enforcement resources would be diverted from the apprehension [arrest] and imprisonment of marijuana offenders to the prevention of much more serious crimes. The huge sums of money that the United States spends each year just to process its marijuana arrests would be available to fund more useful endeavors, such as treatment for substance abusers ... But the decriminalization of marijuana is only a partial solution to the havoc caused by the war on drugs."

–Eric Schlosser, investigative journalist and author

Eric Schlosser, *Reefer Madness: Sex, Drugs, and Cheap Labor in the American Black Market*. Boston, MA: Mariner, 2003, p. 73.

While marijuana has had a rich history in numerous cultures for thousands of years, there are varied accounts of how it made its way into the United States. Some accounts claim the plants were on Christopher Columbus's ships in 1492, while others state that it was grown on hemp plantations after British settlers arrived in Virginia in 1611. While there are many different accounts of how the plant arrived in the United States, it is certain that it became widespread in the 20th century.

The introduction of marijuana to the United States marked the beginning of a long relationship between drug use and American society. Despite all the trends that have come and gone in America; despite all the advancements in the arts and sciences; despite all the changes in political climate, the prevalence of drugs has been a constant in the United States.

The Era of Patent Medicines

Marijuana was not the only illicit, or illegal, drug that found widespread use in America. In the mid-1800s, Chinese immigrants introduced Americans to the custom of smoking opium—a practice the British East India Company profited off of by selling opium to people who were already addicted, despite the fact that it was outlawed by the Chinese government. Chinese immigrants came to the United States for the Gold Rush and to work for the railroads, and the practice of smoking opium soon spread. The practice became so widespread that in 1875, the city of San Francisco, California, outlawed opium parlors. The reason given for this ban was, "Many women and young girls, as well as young men of respectable family, were being induced to visit the Chinese opium-smoking dens, where they were ruined morally and otherwise."[6]

Actually, Americans did not have to sneak into illegal opium dens to use narcotics, and the use of drugs was something that was almost normal—the effects of these drugs were not yet widely known the way they are today. In the 1890s, Sears, Roebuck & Company sold a syringe with cocaine in it for $1.50. This catalog was distributed to millions of homes in the United States. Additionally, patent medicines, or commercially advertised products that were marketed as medicine, were said to eliminate headaches, ease sore throats, and settle queasy stomachs, and they often contained opiates as ingredients. In the late 1890s, Bayer pharmaceutical company began commercially selling heroin. This was even after reports were surfacing that people were developing a tolerance for the drug and seeking more. Bayer used heroin as an ingredient in cough syrups, including those marketed toward children, and this continued until as late as 1912. Additionally, such products as Mrs. Winslow's Soothing Syrup, Dr. McMunn's Elixir of Opium, and Darby's Carminative were sold by salesmen door to door, were available on the shelves of pharmacies, and were advertised widely in the newspapers of the era. Likewise, the companies that manufactured the elixirs and syrups did not have to go through the bother or expense of importing the opium from Asia; during the 19th century, opium was a cash crop in many of the southern U.S. states.

By the early 1900s, many leading physicians of the era concluded that patent medicines were either worthless or harmful. Harvey W. Wiley, a physician and chief chemist for what is now the U.S. Department of Agriculture, became a devoted advocate for outlawing patent medicines. In 1906, Wiley and other experts convinced Congress to pass the Pure Food and Drug Act, which set strict requirements on how medicines could be manufactured and distributed. The act also required drugmakers to list the contents on the bottles. The patent medicine companies, unable to meet the new federal standards, soon went out of business.

The act did not specifically outlaw narcotics, but by then, many of the states had passed antidrug laws of their own. Still, there was pressure on the federal level to take action, mainly because many other countries were struggling with their own narcotics addiction problems. Their leaders hoped an international strategy could be developed. In 1909 and 1911, the United States sent diplomats to international opium conferences, which were called to address the growing drug trade in Asia. Meeting in Belgium in late 1911, the diplomats drafted the 1912 International Opium Convention, which required the member nations to "enact effective laws or regulations for the control of the production and distribution of raw opium."[7] In response, Congress passed the 1914 Harrison Narcotics Act, which placed strict controls on the opiate content of most drugs and made it illegal to sell opiates to people with drug addictions. In addition, medical professionals, such as doctors and pharmacists, had to register and pay a tax in order to prescribe narcotics.

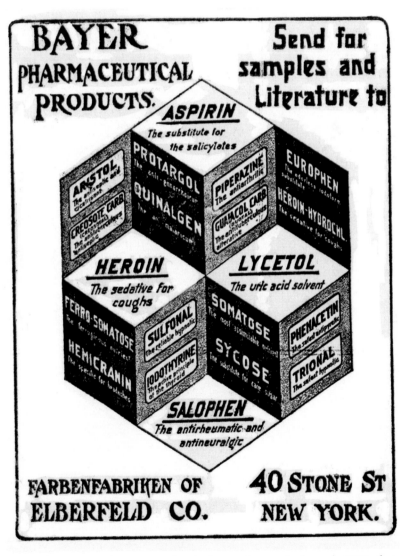

Bayer pharmaceutical company advertised a cough syrup in the early 1900s that contained heroin.

GATEWAY DRUGS

"It is fair to say that the majority of people who use marijuana do not go on to use other substances ... While marijuana often precedes 'harder' drugs in people who do, so does alcohol and even more commonly, nicotine. In that sense, nicotine is a much more common gateway drug."

–Sanjay Gupta, chief medical correspondent for CNN

Quoted in Wayne Drash, "Opioid Commission's Anti-Marijuana Argument Stirs Anger," CNN, November 13, 2017. www.cnn.com/2017/11/13/health/marijuana-opioid-commission/index.html.

The Era of Prohibition

Despite the new law, by 1919, the campaign against illegal drug use in America had become much less of a priority. That was the year the states ratified the 18th Amendment to the U.S. Constitution, outlawing the manufacture and sale of alcoholic beverages. In January 1920, Prohibition went into effect; for the next 13 years, the resources of the federal government were committed to the largely useless task of smashing bootlegging rings, nabbing moonshiners and rum runners (those who smuggled rum, whiskey, and other liquors by sea and land into the United States), and rooting out the thousands of speakeasies (places where alcohol was illegally sold) that were hidden in cities throughout the country. While federal agents hunted down such big-time bootleggers as Al Capone, drug use flourished in America.

In 1930, three years before the end of Prohibition, Congress redirected some of the resources devoted to alcohol enforcement to investigating drug traffickers. In this year, Congress created the Federal Bureau of Narcotics, appointing former Prohibition agent Harry J. Anslinger as the first director. While Anslinger originally thought marijuana was not a big issue, when he was appointed to the Federal Bureau of Narcotics, he soon changed his mind. Anslinger called for a federal law banning the use of marijuana. He traveled the country calling for a war on marijuana and wrote many articles for leading American magazines describing the horrors of the drug. Writing in a 1937 issue of *American Magazine*, Anslinger described what he said was a typical marijuana experience:

> In Los Angeles, Calif., a youth was walking along a downtown street after inhaling a marihuana cigarette. For many addicts, merely a portion of a "reefer" is enough to induce intoxication. Suddenly, for no reason, he decided that someone had threatened to kill him and that his life at that very moment was in danger. Wildly he looked about him. The only person in sight was an aged bootblack [person who shines shoes]. Drug-crazed nerve centers conjured the innocent old shoe-shiner into a destroying monster. Mad with fright, the addict hurried to his room and got a gun. He killed the old man, and then, later, babbled his grief over what had been wanton, uncontrolled murder.[8]

Shocked by these sensationalist—and often completely invented—stories, Congress adopted the Marijuana Tax Act of 1937, which charged heavy fees on importers, regulated distribution, possession, importation, and cultivation of marijuana, and essentially stopped use of the drug. One

Coca-Cola and the Case of the Caffeine Lawsuit

Coca-Cola, one of the most popular soft drinks in America, was originally formulated in 1886 by pharmacist and creator of patent medicines, John Stith Pemberton. The drink was sold at soda fountains and marketed for its supposed benefits for the mind. One early advertisement stated that the beverage "contained the valuable TONIC and NERVE STIMULANT properties of the Coca plant and Cola (or Kola) nuts."[1] As part of the formula, Pemberton included extract of coca leaves, which he imported from South America. Extract of coca leaves is the ingredient of cocaine that provides the illegal drug with its narcotic kick, so early versions of Coca-Cola had trace amounts of cocaine in them.

In 1888, Pemberton sold the formula for the beverage to Asa Candler, who eventually gained

1. Quoted in Kat Eschner, "Coca-Cola's Creator Said the Drink Would Make You Smarter," *Smithsonian*, March 29, 2017. www.smithsonianmag.com/smart-news/coca-colas-creator-said-drink-would-make-you-smarter-180962665/.

complete control of Coca-Cola. While some believe a lawsuit was filed to make the company remove the cocaine ingredient from the formula, it was actually removed voluntarily by the company because public opinion had turned against cocaine. In 1903, Candler had removed nearly all the narcotic from the formula, and it was completely eliminated by 1929, when scientists perfected the method of removing the psychoactive elements from the extract.

The classic Coca-Cola formula did not contain as much cocaine as has been rumored—in fact, it was a very trace amount, and the caffeine content in it was more of a problem for Harvey W. Wiley.

The lawsuit the company faced in 1909 was not because of cocaine; it was because of caffeine. In 1909, Coca-Cola came to the attention of Harvey W. Wiley. Wiley filed a lawsuit against Coca-Cola, charging that the company violated the Pure Food and Drug Act by including caffeine in the formula, and he stated that caffeine was a poison. The case concluded when the judge dismissed it, taking the side of the attorneys for Coca-Cola and stating that the caffeine was not an ingredient that was added, but rather an essential component.

of the provisions of the act was that importers had to register and pay a $24 tax each year. This was a large amount at the time; it would be $406 today. In addition,

> A Marihuana Tax Act Stamp, affixed to each original order form and marked by the revenue collector, insured that proper payments were made. The customs collector maintained custody of imported marijuana at the port of entry until required documents were received, with similar regulations governing marijuana exports. Shipments were subject to searches, seizures and forfeitures if any provisions of the law were not met. Violation of the act resulted in a fine of not more than $2,000 and/or imprisonment for up to five years.[9]

The Federal Bureau of Narcotics eagerly went after drug users and dealers, but with fascism growing in Europe and Japan, the drug war was once again relegated to a low priority. Indeed, Americans were soon engaged in fighting a far different type of war.

Harry J. Anslinger, shown here, originally did not think marijuana was an issue. However, he later changed his mind and declared a war on the drug.

Marijuana and the Vietnam War

Nearly 3 million Americans served in the Vietnam War between 1964 and 1975. Many of them found easy access to drugs and returned to the United States addicted. In 1971, a congressional study found that there were more illicit drugs in Vietnam than cigarettes and chewing gum. Another study suggested that 15 percent of the active soldiers in Vietnam were addicted to heroin.

By far, the most plentiful drug found in Vietnam was marijuana. During the war, military leaders expressed constant concern that discipline in the ranks had eroded because of rampant marijuana use. Vietnam veteran Bob Franco addressed these rumors by saying,

> The only drugs I actually saw men taking was maybe smoking grass. A little marijuana on a three-day stand-down. Now, what I would do is … when we came back for a … three-day rest before going on another operation … I would just say to the men, 'Look, go get drunk … If you're gonna smoke a little dope, don't get caught.' … They'd always show up on the third day straight … because they knew out on the field anybody that wasn't alert, it could cost the other guy's life.[1]

1. "Vietnam: A Television History; Vietnamizing the War (1968–1973); Interview with Robert J. (Bob) Franco," WGBH Media Library & Archives, accessed November 14, 2017. openvault.wgbh.org/catalog/V_74137DF8F9364B388D22FFA7F6C865C6.

Drug Use in the 1960s

Following World War II, a new generation of Americans discovered drugs. Many people in the public eye were known drug users, including writers Jack Kerouac and Allen Ginsberg; movie stars Robert Mitchum and Montgomery Clift; musicians John Coltrane, Charlie Parker, and Chet Baker; and singer Billie Holiday. Meanwhile, some veterans of the Korean War had gotten hooked on a combination of cocaine and heroin known as speedballs. When they returned to the United States, they turned to a prescription drug to feed their habits: methamphetamine, which was known on the streets as "speed" or "crank." In 1963, alarmed at the widespread use of methamphetamine, federal regulators placed strict regulations on the use of the drug, but it was not made illegal until 1970. Those rules hardly dented the speed trade; underground labs soon found ways to make the drug on their own. The drug became the substance of choice for outlaw motorcycle gangs, which took over the manufacture and delivery of speed. One group, the Hell's Angels motorcycle gang, ran an extensive speed distribution ring. According to U.S. attorney G. William Hunter, the gang largely manufactured and mass distributed methamphetamine.

Meanwhile, in the new suburbs that were growing around cities, teenagers and other young people discovered they could experience a mind-numbing rush by sniffing model airplane glue, which they could buy in any hobby store for a few cents. The high-inducing ingredient in the glue is toluene, a solvent that helps the glue dry faster. Doctors started looking at the fad and concluded that it was very dangerous: Glue-sniffing could cause permanent damage to the brain, kidneys, and liver. The model airplane glue industry addressed the problem, and by the late 1960s, manufacturers added irritants to the glue that makes it less desirable to inhale. However, that has not deterred most people who wish to abuse inhalants. Today, there are hundreds of products available on the shelves of supermarkets and hardware stores that contain toluene or other solvents that can provide a high.

Drugs were also finding their way onto college campuses. The 1960s represented an era of great rebellion in American society: The civil rights movement, women's rights movement, and other social changes prompted young people to exert their independence from their parents. Their independence could be found in their hair and clothing styles, their opposition to the Vietnam War, and their desire to use drugs. By the 1960s, marijuana had become a common drug found at most universities in America. Another drug found on campuses was lysergic acid diethylamide (LSD), one of the so-called psychedelic drugs that cause users to experience vivid hallucinations. LSD and similar psychedelic drugs were available in neighborhoods such as Haight-Ashbury in San Francisco and Greenwich Village in New York City. One of the most significant spokesmen for the drug movement in the 1960s was Timothy Leary, a former Harvard University professor who believed LSD expanded the minds of users, opening their consciousness to a variety of new ideas and experiences. In the mid-1960s, he published a book called *Turn On, Tune In, Drop Out*, which was also a phrase he popularized during the same time.

By the late 1960s and early 1970s, drug use was firmly established as a major element of popular culture. Comedians such as George Carlin and the duo Cheech and Chong peppered their acts with drug references. The 1969 film *Easy Rider* tells the story of two drug dealers crossing America on their motorcycles; it was one of the most successful films of the year. On the Broadway stage, the musical *Hair* chronicled the lifestyle of hippie culture, and several songs from the musical described drug use. The show was one of the biggest hits of 1968. Recording stars Arlo Guthrie, Bob Dylan, Jimi Hendrix, and Jefferson Airplane released albums with songs that romanticized their use of drugs. In 1969, more than 400,000 young people attended the Woodstock music festival in upstate New York; drug use was so common there that documentary cameras caught many festival goers and performers using substances, and the stage announcer found it necessary to issue warnings about tainted drugs circulating in the crowd. One of the most successful books of 1971 was Hunter S. Thompson's *Fear and Loathing in Las Vegas*, which tells the story of a sportswriter as he spends a weekend in Las Vegas, Nevada, under the influence of a variety of illegal substances. At one point in the book, the character enters a hotel lobby in the midst of an LSD hallucination and sees nothing but a roomful of lizards. At another point, the character looks up in the sky and sees bats and manta rays. The book was a large success and still influential many years later. In 1998, the film version starring Johnny Depp was released, and the book and movie also influenced the rock band Avenged Sevenfold's song "Bat Country" in 2005.

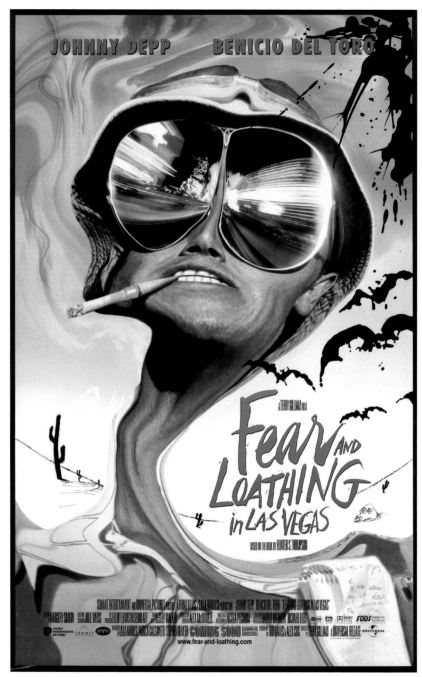

Fear and Loathing in Las Vegas *played a role in making drug use an accepted part of popular culture.*

BREAKING HABITS

"I was on 11 hits of acid a day. I dropped so much acid I'm surprised I can still speak! I'd smoke a bunch of crack, do a bit of meth and just sit there and freak out. Then I'd smoke opium to come down ... I did some [counseling] with the guys [in Linkin Park] and they really opened up and told me how they felt ... I knew that I had a drinking problem, a drug problem and that parts of my personal life were crazy but I didn't realise how much that was affecting the people around me until I got a good dose of 'Here's-what-you're-really-like'. It was a shock. They said I was two people—Chester and that ... guy. I didn't want to be that guy."

—Chester Bennington, former member of the band Linkin Park

Quoted in TeamRock, "Thinking Out Loud: Chester Bennington on Drugs, Success and Going to the Shops," TeamRock, December 6, 2016. teamrock.com/feature/2016-12-06/chester-bennington-interview-linkin-park.

From Discos to Chronic

As the 1970s moved on, the disco music craze gave rise to cocaine use. Celebrities as well as non-famous people gathered at discos, where they took turns inhaling the white powder through rolled-up dollar bills. Additionally, the sign for the popular disco club Studio 54 in New York City included an image of the man in the moon inhaling cocaine from a spoon. As the celebrities gathered around the coke tables, they snorted the drug, oblivious to the fact that their cocaine was being supplied by drug cartels operating in Colombia and other Latin American countries. In his book *Snowblind: A Brief Career in the Cocaine Trade*, writer Robert Sabbag described the small Colombian port town of Santa Maria, from which cocaine was regularly shipped to the United States:

> *Colombian dope, overnight, had become a growth industry. Like every fishing village along the coast, Santa Maria*

Crack versus Cocaine

The terms crack and cocaine cannot be used interchangeably, because they are two different things; however, there are some similarities. Cocaine is a powdered form of hydrochloride salt, while crack is powdered cocaine combined with baking soda and water. After the cocaine is combined with water and baking soda, it is boiled and turns into a solid. This is then broken apart into smaller pieces, which are sold as crack.

The term crack developed because of the crackling sound made when the drug is heated and smoked. In addition, crack and cocaine look different—cocaine is a white powder, while crack is a white, tan, cream, or light brown crystal-like solid. The way each is used also differs—cocaine is generally snorted, while crack is generally smoked.

The effect of each drug differs as much as the appearance and how they are used. Crack is much more concentrated than cocaine is, and therefore, it is highly addictive. In addition, the effects of crack begin in less than 1 minute and last from 30 to 60 minutes. When cocaine is injected, it has this same time frame for the effects. However, when cocaine is snorted, it takes longer to feel the effects—between one and five minutes and lasting between one and two hours.

Crack (left) is made with cocaine (right), which is why it is sometimes called "crack cocaine." However, they are not the same substance.

had come alive, and was throwing all its resources behind the national effort. At least two nights a week the local power plant would shut down while the smugglers, by cover of darkness, took their cash-crop cargoes aboard and shipped out. Police bribes were the savings bonds of the nationwide drive.[10]

In addition, cocaine was making its way into the inner cities, where it was made available in a cheap version known as crack. Wealthy buyers generally preferred ecstasy, ketamine, and what were called club drugs at the time, which dominated the American and European rave scenes. Ecstasy (also known as MDMA for its chemical name, 3,4-methylene-dioxymethamphetamine) and the other club drugs provide users with dreamy, euphoric episodes. They can also prompt hallucinations. Moreover, ketamine and other club drugs, such as Rohypnol and gamma-hydroxybutyrate (GHB), can cause users to fall into drowsy states; as such, they have been used as date-rape drugs. Assailants have distracted people at parties, dropped the pills into their drinks, and then sexually assaulted them. Rohypnol does not change the color or odor of the beverage, so a person would not know they were drugged until it was too late. Those who have been drugged have reported not being able to remember anything starting 20 to 30 minutes after drinking the drugged beverage. In 2003, Andrew Luster, heir to the Max Factor cosmetic company fortune, was convicted on 86 counts of rape and drug charges. Police charged him with lacing the drinks of three women with heavy doses of GHB and then raping them. One of the victims later described her encounter with Luster: "I didn't know I passed out … All I remember is that I was feeling different, and then I woke up the next day in his bed. I was upset and I asked him what was going on, and he said, 'Don't you remember?' Then he said that nothing happened."[11] In 2003, Luster was sentenced to 124 years in prison. However, in 2013, he received a retrial because he argued that he was given bad legal advice and was not properly represented. The judge at his retrial lessened his sentence from the original 124 years down to 50 years.

Andrew Luster, shown here before he started serving time in prison, drugged three women with GHB and then raped them.

Although new drugs such as ecstasy and crack were being introduced, older drugs also remained in use. For example, members of hip-hop culture began using chronic, a particularly powerful strain, or type, of marijuana. In 1992, rapper Dr. Dre released one of the year's most successful albums, titled *The Chronic*. As the name suggests, the album featured many songs praising the qualities of Dr. Dre's drug of choice. Other hip-hop stars who have built their followings largely on their appeal to pot-smoking audiences are Snoop Dogg and Flavor Flav. In 2005, country singer Willie Nelson paid tribute to the late 1970s Jamaican reggae star Bob Marley—whose music was heavily influenced by the marijuana he smoked—by releasing an album titled *Countryman*. Nelson's CD of reggae songs featured marijuana on its cover.

Dr. Dre, shown here, released one of 1992's most successful albums, titled The Chronic *after his drug of choice.*

Meanwhile, mainly in rural areas—but certainly in cities and suburbs as well—amateur drugmakers found a way to make a strong form of methamphetamine, mostly from ingredients available in drugstores and supermarkets. Crystal meth, considered much more powerful than the illegal version of the drug manufactured in the 1960s and 1970s, soon rose to a top place on the list of the nation's most abused drugs.

LESSENED AWARENESS

"The euphoric effects of [ecstasy] can distract users from noticing the physical changes or distress signals from their bodies. With a lessened awareness of pain, it is easy to sustain minor bodily injuries and not be aware of it until the following day."

–Cynthia R. Knowles, author of *Up All Night: A Closer Look at Club Drugs and Rave Culture*

Cynthia R. Knowles, *Up All Night: A Closer Look at Club Drugs and Rave Culture*. New York, NY: Red House, 2001, p. 46.

Tunnels to America

Much of the crystal meth consumed in America "is made in large labs—'superlabs'—in Mexico. There are many small meth labs in operation in the United States, but these mostly serve to feed the habits of the amateur cooks themselves."[12] After the 2001 terrorist attacks on the World Trade Center in New York City and the Pentagon in Washington, D.C., importing crystal meth, marijuana, and other drugs has become much more difficult. Increased vigilance by security officers at airports and border crossings has affected the drug trade. Law enforcement officers watch closely for suspected terrorists, but drug traffickers have been targeted as well. As a result, traffickers have had to find new ways to smuggle drugs into the United States. One such method employed by traffickers is to dig long and elaborate tunnels under the U.S.–Mexico border. Between 1990 and 2016, authorities discovered more than 180 tunnels, some thousands of feet in length, dug beneath the U.S. borders with Mexico and Canada. One of the longest tunnels, which was 2,400 feet (731.5 m), was discovered in early 2006. On the Mexican side, entry to the tunnel was gained through a small warehouse in Tijuana. On the American side, the drug traffickers emerged from the tunnel into a 48,225 square foot (4,480.2 sq m) warehouse in Otay Mesa, California. In addition, the tunnel itself was complex, with lights, a ventilation system to allow airflow, and other enhancements. The *San Diego Union Tribune* reported, "The tunnel from Tijuana goes north for hundreds of feet. Inside the United States, it intersects with a second tunnel coming in from the Otay Mesa warehouse. The main tunnel continues for about 100 feet before coming to a dead end."[13]

Prescription Painkillers

Drug agents may be fighting larger drug trafficking rings to try to stop these dangerous substances from getting into the hands of the public, but it is not just drugs such as heroin or cocaine that are making their way into society. For some, the substances they are addicted to are found in the medicine cabinet. According to the Centers for Disease Control and Prevention (CDC), "The epidemic of opiate addiction, which has left roughly 2 million Americans addicted to narcotic painkillers, has claimed more than 183,000 lives since 1999."[14]

While there has been a heroin epidemic in the United States for years, some of that epidemic began with prescription painkillers. A person may be prescribed them after an injury or surgery, and eventually they build up a tolerance to the medication if they are on it for a long period of time. When a person builds a tolerance, it means the same amount they have been taking may not be helping them anymore. They may increase the dose and find that they need a refill sooner. Alternatively, their prescription may run out, and they need to find other means of handling their pain and turn to a cheaper opioid alternative—heroin.

However, while addiction to prescription painkillers partly has a hand in creating the heroin epidemic, not all people who use prescription painkillers turn to harder drugs such as heroin, and not all people who are prescribed these pills become addicted. A person may take their exact prescribed amount and never refill the prescription; in fact, according to NIDA, the majority of people who are prescribed painkillers use them responsibly. For this reason, and because many people who take them do so for chronic (long-term), intense pain that does not respond to weaker painkillers, making opioids completely illegal is not a good option. People who are addicted to them will find ways to get them even if they are illegal, and people who need them to legitimately manage pain will suffer. However, due to the high possibility of addiction to painkillers such as OxyContin and the possibility of the patient turning to other drugs, researchers are looking into new types of painkillers. According to a July 2017 report by the National Academies of Science, Engineering, and Medicine, at least 8 percent of patients who are prescribed opioid painkillers become addicted, and 15 to 26 percent become dependent, which means they require the drug to function.

Where did this addiction and dependence start? In large part, it began in the emergency department of hospitals. According to a study in the United States between 2001 and 2010, emergency room visits in which the patient was prescribed an opioid painkiller rose from 21 percent to 31 percent. However, in a study released in November 2017, "researchers found that a cocktail of two non-addictive, over-the-counter drugs relieved pain just as well as—and maybe a little better than—a trio of opioid pain medications widely prescribed under such circumstances."[15] This new study adds extra information to the recent discussion about how much opioid painkillers are prescribed and whether they need be prescribed at all for short-term pain.

The Effects of Drug Use

While drugs lure people in with a short amount of euphoria, the long-term and short-term effects are hefty prices to pay for those few minutes of euphoria. Most drugs, such as heroin, cocaine, and meth, can forever alter the user's life. Whether it is a hard-to-beat addiction, a hole in the septum (the tissue that divides the nostrils) from repeated cocaine inhalation, or the severe tooth decay and gum disease that is commonly referred to as "meth mouth," repeated drug use can take an extreme toll on a person. Drug abuse can also cause death; drugs are the leading cause of death for Americans under the age of 50. According to data compiled by the *New York Times*, 52,404 Americans died from drug overdoses in 2015 alone. In 2016, that figure rose 22 percent, with about 64,000 Americans dying from drug overdoses in that year. Between 2013 and 2016, the amount of deaths from fentanyl overdoses rose 540 percent.

Drugs in the Entertainment Industry

Drug abuse contributes to thousands of deaths a year, and celebrities are no exception. Some do it because they think the effects sound like fun, although they may quickly find that they are caught up in an addiction that is not fun at all. Others do it as a way to escape the pressures of celebrity life. While it may seem as though the fame and fortune that come with being a celebrity makes for a perfect life, the reality is that constantly being in the public eye and having their appearance and actions criticized can be very stressful. While some celebrities have overcome a drug addiction and talked about their struggles, some have not been able to. Actress and singer Demi Lovato has spoken of her addiction, stating she would sneak out to use drugs and use other people's urine for drug tests. At one point, she used cocaine and Xanax, started to choke, and at that moment, realized how easy it would be to overdose.

Iron Man actor Robert Downey Jr. famously battled with cocaine and heroin addiction. In 1996, he was arrested for possession of cocaine and heroin as well as driving under the influence of drugs and alcohol. He spent about one year in prison and was later released on parole and probation for these arrests. However, even his prison stay was not enough to make him stop using drugs because drug addiction is a disease, not a choice. He later relapsed and checked himself into a rehabilitation facility in 2001. As of 2018, he is still not using drugs and is also one of the largest stars in the movie industry, thanks to his role as Iron Man in the Marvel Cinematic Universe (MCU).

Robert Downey Jr., shown here, battled with cocaine and heroin addiction. However, he beat his addictions and became one of the most successful actors in Hollywood with his role as Iron Man in the Marvel Cinematic Universe.

While Demi Lovato and Robert Downey Jr. are success stories of sobriety, other celebrities have not been so lucky. *Glee* star Corey Monteith battled drug addiction from the age of 13. In 2013, he died at the age of 31 from a mixture of heroin and alcohol; just three months before his death, he had achieved sobriety in a rehabilitation facility.

Actor Heath Ledger was found dead in his New York City apartment in early 2008. Already one of the brightest young stars in the movie industry, especially with his famous role as the Joker in *The Dark Knight*, the 28-year-old Australian suffered from bodily pain as a result of taking on physically challenging roles. He also had difficulty sleeping and was clinically depressed. Shortly before Ledger died, he was known to be consuming no fewer than six prescription medications. The mixture of drugs proved deadly: They slowed down the functions of his organs, particularly his lungs. "His breathing probably got slower and slower until it stopped altogether," said pathologist Michael Hunter. As a result, Hunter said, Ledger died of "poly-drug intoxication."[16]

Heath Ledger, shown here, was found dead in 2008 due to a combination of multiple prescription pills.

In other victims, drugs take their toll much more slowly, gradually destroying the vital functions of the brain and body. When jazz musician Charlie Parker was found dead of a drug overdose in 1955, the coroner estimated his age to be between 50 and 60. In reality, Parker was only 34 years old.

Neurotransmitters and Drugs

Drugs affect many parts of the body, but the primary organ that is impacted by narcotics is the brain. The brain is composed of millions of cells called neurons. Each neuron emits an electrical impulse that carries the brain's messages, such as instructing a foot to take a step, the lips to form words, or the fingers to grasp a pencil. Within each neuron are a series of stems that act as pathways for the impulses. The larger stems are axons; at the end of the axons are smaller stems called dendrites. The impulse travels along the axon and into the dendrite. When the impulse reaches the end of the dendrite, it must leap over a tiny space called a synapse on its way to the next dendrite. To enable the electrical impulse to make the leap, the brain produces chemicals known as neurotransmitters, which carry the messages between the brain cells. On the end of each neuron's dendrite is a group of molecules called receptors, which accept specific neurotransmitters and transmit the impulse into the neuron and over the next synapse. Not all neurotransmitters carry messages; some prevent unwanted messages from passing between the neurons.

The method the brain employs to communicate with the rest of the body is well synchronized, delicate, and spontaneous. When drugs are introduced into the brain's system of communication, the results can be helpful to the user. For example, prescription painkillers, when used properly, can block the neurotransmitters that carry messages of pain to the rest of the body. Drugs, however, also can be quite disruptive, affecting mood and emotion or motor activity—how a person walks, talks, or operates machinery.

Drugs affect neurotransmitters. Sometimes drugs cause the brain cells to produce too many neurotransmitters, which overwhelm the brain with information. For example, the neurotransmitter dopamine controls movement. When the brain is overloaded with dopamine, a person may stumble and lose coordination. That is why people who abuse drugs should not drive while they are under the influence of substances.

NEURON

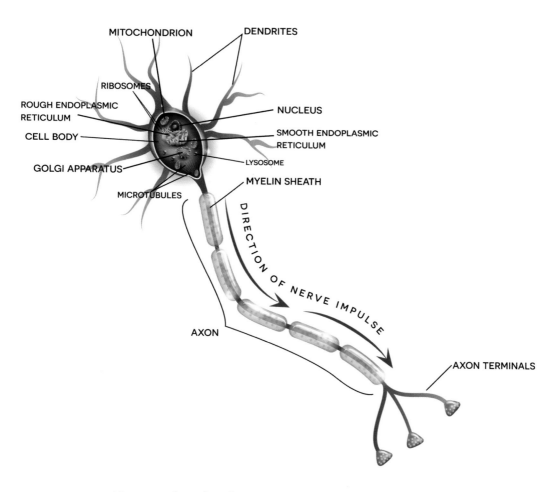

Neurons send impulses along axons and dendrites. The brain produces neurotransmitters to carry these messages between brain cells.

Neurotransmitters can also alter moods and produce feelings of pleasure. In addition to motor activity, dopamine also controls cognitive thinking, motivation, emotion, and feelings of pleasure—all functions that can be affected by drugs. Some drugs spark the brain to produce more dopamine, enhancing pleasure. That is why drug abusers often feel joyful and silly, even though they are stumbling on their feet or crashing into furniture. Methamphetamine and cocaine produce an overwhelming amount of dopamine. "It produces a marked decrease in hunger, an indifference to pain, and is reputed to be the most potent [powerful] anti-fatigue agent known," wrote Jerome H. Jaffe, who was chief of President Richard Nixon's drug programs. "The user enjoys a feeling of great muscular strength and increased mental capacity and greatly overestimates his capabilities. The euphoria is accompanied by generalized ... stimulation."[17] For this reason, Adolf Hitler encouraged Nazi soldiers to take crystal meth to make them feel stronger and stay awake longer.

Sometimes drugs block neurotransmitters by affecting the receptors. In each brain cell, the neurotransmitters act as keys that unlock specific receptors, which accept the messages and pass them on to the next cell. However, some drugs mimic neurotransmitters, blocking the natural chemicals from entering the receptors. Instead, the drugs take the place of the neurotransmitters and enter the receptors. LSD, for example, mimics serotonin. Serotonin regulates mood, sleep, pain, emotion, and appetite. Instead of receiving serotonin, the brain absorbs a dose of LSD and its hallucination-causing qualities.

The chemical delta-9-tetrahydrocannabinol (THC) is the psychoactive component of marijuana, which means it is the ingredient that delivers the "high." THC is known to block serotonin and take its place in the brain's serotonin receptors. That is why marijuana smokers undergo a change in their moods—most users experience dreamy, euphoric highs. Marijuana users also often notice a change in their appetites, which is commonly called the "munchies." The reason for this is that

THC fits into receptors that are part of the brain's natural endocannabinoid system, which helps to control emotions, memory, pain

sensitivity and appetite. Our brains typically produce their own chemicals (called cannabinoids) that fit into these same receptors, so by mimicking their activity, THC can artificially alter the same factors in dramatic ways … [THC] mimics sensations felt when we're deprived of food … In other words, THC appears to give us the munchies by convincing our brains that we're starving.[18]

The psychoactive component in marijuana mimics the sensations of food deprivation, causing users to consume a lot of food because their body thinks it is starving.

CAUSE AND EFFECT

"The long-term health effects of chronic cannabis use, and marijuana's role as a 'gateway' to the use of other illegal drugs, are issues surrounded by controversy. Marijuana does not create a physical dependence in its users, although it does create a psychological dependence in some ... People who smoke marijuana are more likely to experiment later with other psychoactive drugs, but a direct cause-and-effect relationship has never been established. Marijuana's potential role as a 'stepping stone' to other drugs is most likely determined by cultural, not pharmacological factors."

—Eric Schlosser, investigative journalist and author

Eric Schlosser, *Reefer Madness: Sex, Drugs, and Cheap Labor in the American Black Market.* Boston, MA: Mariner, 2003, p. 17.

Addiction and the Brain

Eventually, the brain will grow accustomed to the new sensations provided by most drugs and will create a desire within the user to want more. Most people possess a natural tendency to want more of what gives them pleasure. Therefore, many people who have tried heroin, cocaine, meth, or other drugs return for a second dose because of the pleasure they received from their first experiences with the substance.

When the brain rewards the body, it releases dopamine. For example, when a person eats their favorite food, the brain will respond by releasing a small amount of dopamine, giving the eater pleasure for having consumed a tasty food. Some drugs prompt the body to release dopamine in amounts 10 times the normal quantity. Therefore, the rush of pleasure associated with drug abuse can be enormous.

The pleasurable experience gained through drugs will also last much longer than the feeling of pleasure produced through a natural release of dopamine. For instance, the rush of pleasure someone may receive from eating their favorite food may last no longer than a few seconds or a few minutes, but when prompted by drugs, the feelings of pleasure can last much longer. The high produced by cocaine can last more than 30 minutes. Abusers of methamphetamine can expect to stay high and euphoric for 8 to 24 hours. "The effect of such a powerful reward strongly motivates people to take drugs again and again," according to NIDA. "This is why scientists sometimes say drug abuse is something we learn to do very, very well."[19]

OVEREMPHASIS ON MARIJUANA

"If we can get a child to 20 without using marijuana, there is a 98 percent chance that the child will never become addicted to any drug. While it may come across as an overemphasis on marijuana, you don't wake up when you're 25 and say, 'I want to slam meth!'"

—Scott Burns, former White House Deputy Drug Czar in the Office of National Drug Control Policy

Quoted in David J. Jefferson, "America's Most Dangerous Drug," *Newsweek*, August 8, 2005. www.newsweek.com/americas-most-dangerous-drug-117493.

The frequent use of drugs often creates an addiction in the user. Over time, the brain comes to rely on the pleasurable sensations provided by drugs, creating a craving in the user for larger and more frequent doses. Olivia Gordon, an ecstasy user, found that after she started using the drug, a single dose of it was no longer capable of getting her high. "Each time I took a pill, the high was getting less glorious,"[20] she wrote.

In addition, when drugs induce the brain to create more dopamine, the brain stops producing dopamine on its own. That means the brain requires drugs to carry out functions it formerly did on its own. According to NIDA:

This is why a person who abuses drugs eventually feels flat, lifeless, and depressed, and is unable to enjoy things that were previously pleasurable. Now, the person needs to keep taking drugs again and again just to try and bring his or her dopamine function back up to normal—which only makes the problem worse, like a vicious cycle. Also, the person will often need to take larger amounts of the drug to produce the familiar dopamine high—an effect known as tolerance.[21]

The National Institutes of Health (NIH) and NIDA regard drug addiction as a disease of the brain. As a person takes more and more drugs, the way the brain works will change. Its functions will become abnormal. Brain imaging studies performed on long-term drug abusers show that, in many cases, the brain has actually undergone physical changes. After years of drug abuse, the parts of the brain that control judgment, decision making, learning, memory, and behavioral control have shown deterioration.

The saddest fact about addiction is that, in time, most people do arrive at the realization that drugs are bad for them, and yet it is very difficult for them to stop abusing substances. An addiction is a repetitive behavior in spite of negative consequences— it is the desire to do something even though a person knows it is bad for them.

As their drug use continues, people with an addiction may find themselves experiencing difficulty concentrating, solving problems, and maintaining their short- and long-term memories. Numerous studies have looked at the effects of drugs on cognitive development, and most have concluded that drugs harm the brain. Inhalants, for example, contain harsh industrial chemicals that were never intended to be absorbed directly into the body. When inhaled, these chemicals enter the bloodstream and flow through the brain, where they become lodged in the myelin—the fatty coating of tissue that protects each neuron. Eventually they break down the myelin, which could damage the neurons or prevent them from transmitting messages. As a result, the drug abuser may find it harder to remember things.

Researchers at the University of Edinburgh studied the brains of 34 methadone and heroin users and compared the results with the brains of 16 people who had died at a young age but had never used drugs. The heroin and methadone users had an average age of 26, and some of them had died at age 17. According to the researchers' findings, *young drug abusers were up to three times more likely to suffer brain damage, than those who did not use drugs. The drug abusers meanwhile sustained a level of brain damage normally only seen in much older people and similar to the early stages of Alzheimer's.*[22]

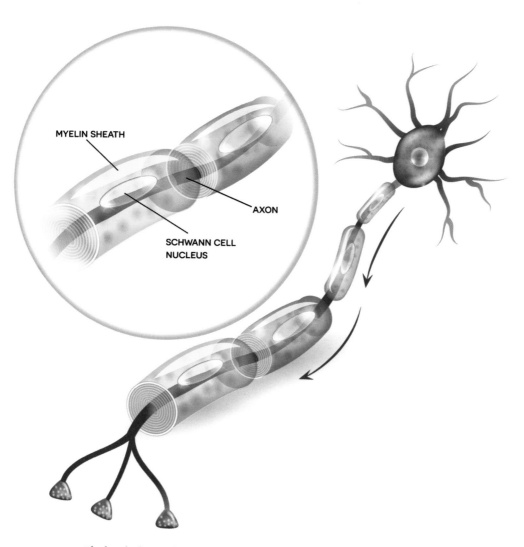

MYELIN SHEATH

AXON

SCHWANN CELL NUCLEUS

The harsh chemicals of inhalants can break down the myelin that surrounds each neuron.

The study showed that heroin causes some areas of the brain to become severely damaged or die as well as prematurely age by 50 to 60 years.

As for marijuana, many studies have linked it to long-term memory loss, and it can also permanently alter short-term memory. In 2005, a five-year study at Johns Hopkins University in Baltimore, Maryland, found that marijuana causes a reduction in the blood vessels that feed the brain. With less blood in the brain, the brain deteriorates and has more difficulty carrying out its functions. "In the long-term, one might see cognitive difficulties, such as problems with memory and thinking,"[23] said Ronald Herning, the Johns Hopkins physician who conducted the study. The University of Lausanne, Switzerland, also conducted a study that was published in 2016 on how marijuana affects short-term memory. The study examined the marijuana habits of 3,400 Americans throughout a 25-year period and found that those who smoked marijuana daily for five years or more had poorer memory in their middle ages than those who did not smoke marijuana at all or those who smoked less marijuana. The more marijuana a person smoked, the worse they performed on the memory tests given at the end of the study. For example,

Let's say we have two groups of 10 people each. You tell each of them a list of 15 words and ask them to memorize them. Then 25 minutes later, you ask them to recall all the words to the best of their ability. The first group consists of 10 people who don't smoke pot or only do so occasionally. Let's say on average, people in this group would be able to remember nine out of the 15 words.

The second group consists of people who smoked pot every single day over a period of five years. On average, they'd be able to recall 8.5 out of the 15 words.

That doesn't seem like a huge cognitive difference, and by and large it's not. But multiply that by every five marijuana years of exposure, and the gap can grow.[24]

The study did state, however, that not many people smoke this much marijuana—out of all their participants, only 8 percent, or

311 people, smoked this much. However, even though so few people actually smoke that much, it shows that too much of anything, whether it is junk food or marijuana, can be bad for a person.

CHANGES IN THE BRAIN

"Many people don't understand why or how other people become addicted to drugs. They may mistakenly think that those who use drugs lack moral principles or willpower and that they could stop their drug use simply by choosing to. In reality, drug addiction is a complex disease, and quitting usually takes more than good intentions or a strong will. Drugs change the brain in ways that make quitting hard, even for those who want to."

—National Institute on Drug Abuse

"Understanding Drug Use and Addiction," National Institute on Drug Abuse, revised August 2016. www.drugabuse.gov/publications/drugfacts/understanding-drug-use-addiction.

Addiction and the Body

While the brain changes over time, the body does as well. Most illicit drugs contain ingredients that affect other parts of the body, in both the long and short term. For example, a short-term effect of the hallucinogenic drug phencyclidine (PCP), which is also known as angel dust, is a rise in the user's body temperature. That condition often prompts PCP users to strip off their clothes—some have been arrested by police as they wandered naked and disoriented through the streets. In the long term, PCP users have suffered memory loss, speech difficulties, weight loss, reduced blood pressure, respiratory problems, and kidney failure.

Other drugs also attack the kidneys as well as other organs. For example, the toxic ingredients of inhalants that break down the myelin surrounding the neurons also attack other parts of the body. When used over an extended period of time, inhalants can damage the heart, kidneys, and lungs.

The manufacture of methamphetamine requires the use of acids and solvents, which illegal labs obtain from hardware stores and supermarkets. Drain cleaner and acetone (an ingredient found in nail polish remover and paint thinners) are common components of crystal meth. When people who use crystal meth ingest those substances, they risk damage to the throat and esophagus, which are irritated by the destructive chemicals. Crystal meth also rots teeth—a condition known as "meth mouth."

Cocaine is generally associated with septum perforation, which is when the tissue that separates the nostrils is eroded away and forms a hole. However, cocaine can also cause extreme damage to the roof of the mouth, leaving a hole and affecting drinking, eating, and speaking. The roof of the mouth

> has a fragile blood supply, and this is shut off by cocaine use. This process is called vasoconstriction (closing off of blood vessels). When the blood vessels constrict, the blood supply is compromised, delivering less oxygen to the tissues of the

The Dangers of Kratom

The kratom plant has been used to slow the effects of withdrawal from opioids. Found in Malaysia and Thailand, the powdered form of the herbal supplement can be used in beverages such as tea to ease withdrawal effects. Some people who suffer from chronic pain have also used the powder. However, in 2016, the Drug Enforcement Administration (DEA) was considering banning it for two years because of the effects—essentially, it mimics an opioid to the point that the DEA sees it as a threat to public safety. However, the ban never fully took effect, and in 2017, the U.S. Food and Drug Administration (FDA) joined in and issued a public health advisory on the herbal supplement.

Scott Gottlieb, the commissioner of the FDA, warned that the supplement could be addictive and expressed plans to meet with the DEA to determine a drug schedule, or classification, for kratom. The possible addictive quality is not the only thing the FDA and DEA are worried about. Gottlieb's advisory statement cited

1. Nick Wing, "Feds Prepare for a New War on Kratom, An Herbal Drug Many Swear By," *Huffington Post*, November 14, 2017. www.huffingtonpost.com/entry/fda-kratom-regulation_us_5a0b465be4b00a6eece4c9e0

2. Quoted in Wing, "Feds Prepare for a New War."

3. Matt Simon and Nick Stockton, "Kratom: The Bitter Plant that Could Help Opioid Addicts—If the DEA Doesn't Ban It," *Wired*, November 30, 2016. www.wired.com/2016/11/kratom-bitter-plant-help-opioid-addicts-dea-doesnt-ban/

"36 deaths associated with kratom-containing products and a tenfold increase in calls involving kratom to U.S. poison control centers from 2010 to 2015."[1] In addition, Gottlieb suggested kratom "could actually 'expand the opioid epidemic.'"[2]

More research into kratom is needed, but with DEA plans to place it in the Schedule I category of drugs, which contains some of the most dangerous and addictive drugs, this research will be hard to do. Some people have found that kratom helps their opioid withdrawal symptoms, but "[s]cientists know practically nothing about kratom–how its compounds work in concert [together], what it can actually treat, how addictive it might be, what counts as a safe dose. And certainly not enough to back up all the life-changing claims extolled in public comments [on websites]."[3] As with all medical concerns, it is best to consult a doctor before trying any "cures," especially when the positive notes about that "cure" come from a few comments on a website and the "cure" has not been thoroughly researched by scientists.

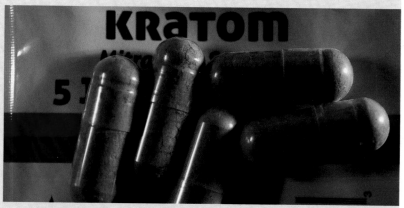

In 2016, the DEA expressed concerns over kratom, the herbal supplement shown here. In 2017, the FDA issued a public health advisory on the supplement, citing 36 kratom-related deaths between 2010 and 2015.

palate. With low oxygen, the palate lining begins to die and shrink away leaving a [hole].[25]

Acetone, an ingredient found in nail polish remover, is a common ingredient in crystal meth.

In addition, the hole is not able to heal on its own and requires the user to first stop using all drugs and then see a surgeon to have the hole repaired.

Some studies have also compared the health effects of marijuana with those of tobacco use. For decades, physicians have warned smokers about the cancer-causing ingredients of tobacco products. The possibility of marijuana causing lung cancer has been a harder subject to study for a few reasons. First of all, it has been illegal in many places for such a long time that it is not easy for researchers to gather information about the use of the drug. Additionally, many people in past lung cancer studies smoked cigarettes as well as marijuana, making it hard for researchers to know how much of the risk was from tobacco and how much was from marijuana. According to the American Cancer Society, some reasons marijuana use may increase risk of lung cancer include:

- *Marijuana smoke contains tar and many of [the same] cancer-causing substances that are in tobacco smoke. (Tar is the sticky, solid material that remains after burning, which is thought to contain most of the harmful substances in smoke.)*

- *Marijuana cigarettes (joints) are typically smoked all the way to the end, where tar content is the highest.*

- *Marijuana is inhaled very deeply and the smoke is held in the lungs for a long time, which gives any cancer-causing substances more opportunity to deposit in the lungs.*

- *Because marijuana is still illegal in many places, it may not be possible to control what other substances it might contain.*[26]

STIGMAS PREVENT TREATMENT

"Many people who die from an overdose struggle with an opioid use disorder or other substance use disorder, and unfortunately misconceptions surrounding these disorders have contributed to harmful stigmas that prevent individuals from seeking evidence-based treatment."

–President Barack Obama, proclamation instituting the first Prescription Opioid and Heroin Epidemic Awareness Week in September 2016

Barack Obama, "Presidential Proclamation—Prescription Opioid and Heroin Epidemic Awareness Week, 2016," The White House, September 16, 2016. www.whitehouse.gov/the-press-office/2016/09/16/presidential-proclamation-prescription-opioid-and-heroin-epidemic.

Combating Substance Abuse in College

According to the Alcohol and Other Drug Assistance Program (ADAP) of Rutgers University, around 30 percent of college students have a substance-use disorder. In response, more and more colleges in the United States are developing college recovery programs (CRPs) to help students stay clean and stay in college. According to the *Chicago Tribune*,

> *Programs typically include mental health and substance abuse counseling, addiction support group meetings, peer-to-peer support, and a wide variety of substance-free programs and social activities that help students bond and sustain their sobriety in the "abstinence-hostile environment" of college campuses.*[1]

In addition, many programs also have on-campus housing that does not allow drugs or alcohol and allows college students to support each other beyond the scheduled events or counseling.

Between 2012 and 2017, the number of CRPs rose from 35 to more than 150, and around 50 of those include special on-campus housing. CRPs have been shown to have quite an impact on students' lives. They allow students to get and stay sober, and they do not isolate them from the college atmosphere. While the purpose of college is to earn a degree, there is also a social aspect to it—students entering college want to make new friends and have fun. The CRPs allow students to do just that; they have friends who help them stay sober, and being part of this community helps them stay on track to reach their goals of not only staying sober but also earning a degree. One student who participated in his school's CRP said, "You have friends who understand your situation ... people who watch out for you and can give you that social life everyone is looking for in college [without drugs and alcohol]."[2] Thanks to this student's CRP, he has been sober for 6 years as of 2017, earned his bachelor's and master's degrees, and helps nonprofit organizations that are dedicated to substance abuse recovery.

1. Claire Altschuler, "Colleges Use Sober Dorms to Combat Alcohol, Drug Addiction," *Chicago Tribune*, October 13, 2017. www.chicagotribune.com/lifestyles/sc-fam-sober-dorms-1017-story.html.
2. Quoted in Altschuler, "Colleges Use Sober Dorms to Combat Alcohol, Drug Addiction."

Overdose

The most publicized effect of drug abuse is death from an overdose. "Overdose" simply means taking too much of any drug, and not all overdoses are fatal; for instance, taking more than the recommended amount of an over-the-counter painkiller such as ibuprofen will generally not kill someone, but if enough is taken, it could cause severe pain and damage to the person's body. Fatal overdoses are more likely with dangerous drugs such as heroin, cocaine, and opioids. A number of celebrities—such as Chris Farley, Corey Monteith, Philip Seymour Hoffman, Prince, and Carrie Fisher—all had drugs in their system when they died. Each year, the number of deaths due to drugs climbs; between 2015 and 2016 alone, it rose 22 percent. What happens during an overdose varies depending on the drug that was taken as well as a few other factors, including whether the person has relapsed; whether they have mixed drugs (for example, opioids with alcohol); or whether they have taken the drugs in high doses. One of the largest risks of overdose is relapse—if a person relapses, they often take the amount they were previously using before rehabilitation. As the person's body is not used to this high amount anymore, it puts even more stress on the body. In addition, a person who is overdosing is rarely aware that it is happening. However, others may notice, and they should get help for the person immediately because it is a life-or-death situation. Some signs of an overdose others may observe include extremely slowed breathing (fewer than 10 breaths per minute), nausea, drowsiness, vomiting, and cold hands.

In the case of opioids, such as heroin, the first stage is that the drug spreads throughout the body. It enters the heart and lungs, where the blood is flushed with oxygen before returning to the heart. The next pump of the heart pushes opioid-rich blood throughout the body, and when the drug hits the brain, a euphoric feeling follows. According to an article on the website Vice, "Once the opioid molecules are ferried across the blood-brain barrier, they enter a section of the brain at the center of your reward circuitry called the nucleus accumbens, where the happiness hormone dopamine is produced." Once there, the drug attaches to the gamma-aminobutyric acid (GABA) neurotransmitters. Vice continued, "Imagine GABA as a dam: They make sure our dopamine doesn't overflow, which can cause agitation and paranoia. Opioid particles blow that dam open, and let dopamine spill over into the bloodstream, creating a feeling of bliss, way beyond what our GABA cells would normally allow us to experience."[27]

At this point, breathing starts to slow. The user feels relaxed and tired, which is commonly referred to as "on the nod" with drugs such as heroin. As the user becomes more relaxed, the opioid starts shutting down important body functions such as heart rate and breathing because the drug suppresses normal neurological signals. The oxygen level may become so low that the heart starts beating irregularly, and the person may go into cardiac arrest, which is when the heart starts beating out of rhythm and the normal pumping action of the heart is disrupted. At this point, the heart is unable to pump blood to vital areas such as the lungs, brain, and other organs, and the person may become unconscious.

If the person does not go into cardiac arrest, body functions start to shut down. Because the drug overwhelms the brain, the body does not receive signals to breathe, and the brain becomes damaged from lack of oxygen. After four minutes of oxygen deprivation in the brain, permanent brain damage can occur. Additionally, the person may choke, foam at the mouth, or have a seizure from lack of oxygen to the brain. However, a drug called Narcan has the ability to reverse an overdose if it is administered in time. Narcan can be administered by a shot or nasal spray, which starts working in minutes, or by an IV, which works within seconds.

CHAPTER 3

Societal Impact

Drug abuse is not an isolated thing that only the user experiences. While drugs have a profound effect on the body, they also affect the user's relationships and society. Families and friends are affected deeply by the drug abuse of their loved one, and even society is greatly affected by drug abuse. More than 80,000, or 46.3 percent, of inmates in prison are there because of drug convictions. In addition, sharing heroin needles can spread the human immunodeficiency virus (HIV) and AIDS, and the foster care system even feels the effects of drug abuse. According to NIDA, "Directly or indirectly, every community is affected by drug abuse and addiction, as is every family. Drugs take a tremendous toll on our society at many levels."[28]

The Foster Care Crisis

The rise in drug abuse, especially opioids, has hit the foster care system especially hard. Children are removed from their homes because of the parents' substance-abuse disorder, and some children are born addicted to drugs because their mother used them while she was pregnant. Children who are born addicted to opioids require methadone shots daily in order to manage the painful withdrawal symptoms, which include vomiting, sweating, muscle aches, and abdominal cramping. For example, in Maine, more than 1,000 children are born addicted to drugs each year. According to the NIH, "children exposed to opiates during pregnancy suffer from behavior and attention problems. Such children require therapy and often specially licensed and trained foster families, and states say they are struggling to recruit foster families to house them."[29]

In Maine in 2016, more than 1,800 children were in foster care, which was a 45 percent increase since 2011. Maine is not alone in these trends. These kinds of statistics are echoed in foster care systems throughout the United States. Because of the heroin epidemic and addiction to prescription pills, more and more children are being placed into the state's custody.

Between 2011 and 2015, children in foster care in Massachusetts increased 19 percent. The *Washington Post* reported in 2017, "Foster-care experts say that as the drug epidemic has intensified during the past two years, another rush of children has entered the system. State budgets are stretched, social workers are overloaded, and not enough families are willing to provide children with temporary homes."[30]

Some states have had to change laws and issue emergency pleas to change this crisis in the foster care system. Vermont and New Hampshire, for example, have had to change their laws in order to remove children from homes where parents are addicted to drugs or adjust the budget so more social workers can be hired. Ohio, Alaska, and Kansas, on the other hand, have "issued emergency pleas for more people to become foster parents and take neglected children, many of them infants, into their homes."[31] Ohio, especially, is having a foster care crisis, with more than 9,900 children in foster care—half of whom were taken from their homes because of parental drug abuse. In addition, case workers in Ohio are finding it difficult to place children with relatives because "[b]y the time the children get to foster care, they report, many of the adults in their extended family are addicted to opiates, too."[32]

According to the Pew Charitable Trusts, this increase of children in foster care can be attributed to a few things, such as stricter reporting of child abuse and federal laws that require hospitals to notify child protective services if children have been exposed to illicit substances prior to being born. However, even considering these points, help is still needed in either a different response to the drug-addiction epidemic, a change in the way the foster care system functions, or both.

NOT ALONE

"You feel alone in this, ashamed, like no other family is affected by this, but we learned that's just not true in this county. So many families like ours are going through the same thing."

—Richard Gauthier, whose son was addicted to methamphetamine

Quoted in Tamara Koehler, "Teens and Their Families Struggle to Overcome Meth's Grip," *Ventura County Star,* October 21, 2007. www.venturacountystar.com/news/2007/oct/21/teens-families-struggle-with-meth.

Britt and Garrett Reid

Many families in the United States are affected by the substance-use disorders of their loved ones. Sometimes it happens to a family that people would least suspect of being affected by drug abuse—a family such as the Reids.

In 2007, the sons of Andy Reid, a head coach in the National Football League (NFL), were arrested on drug-related charges in separate incidents. As the story unfolded, it became apparent that Britt and Garrett Reid had both suffered from long-term addictions. For months, the stories of the two Reid sons dominated the media in Philadelphia, Pennsylvania, as well as the rest of the country.

The incidents began on January 30, 2007, when police responded to a road-rage case on a suburban Philadelphia street in which Britt Reid, who was 22 years old at the time, was alleged to have pointed a gun at another driver. Inside Britt's car, police found a .45-caliber pistol; a shotgun; ammunition; and quantities of cocaine, marijuana, and prescription painkillers. Later that day, police pursued a car driving at a high rate of speed, which ended in a crash that injured another driver. When police finally caught up with the car they had been chasing, they found Britt's 24-year-old brother, Garrett, at the wheel. Inside Garrett's car, police found quantities of heroin, pills, and a scale for weighing drugs. That day, Garrett tested positive for heroin and was charged with driving under the influence.

Both of the coach's sons got into trouble again after these incidents. While awaiting trial on bail, Britt used drugs and crashed his car in the parking lot of a sporting goods store. Meanwhile, Garrett was charged with attempting to smuggle drugs into prison while awaiting trial. After his second arrest, Garrett resolved to stay clean. In November, Britt and Garrett were each sentenced; Britt was sentenced to eight to twenty-three months in prison, and Garett was sentenced to two to twenty-three months in prison. The judge suggested that the Reid home may not have been the best place for Garrett and Britt to stay once they were released from prison because of the prescription and illegal drugs that were found there during police searches.

Throughout the months that their cases were pending, Andy Reid found himself under tremendous pressure to

What Not to Say

Drug addiction is a highly stigmatized disorder and one that people may judge others for quickly. Additionally, sometimes people mean well, but things they say in an attempt to be helpful may actually be hurtful to the person struggling with addiction. The following are 10 things that should never be said to a person who is recovering from a substance-use disorder:

1. "But you don't seem like a drug addict." ...

2. "We're all addicts, when you get right down to it. I'm totally addicted to the Internet." ...

3. "Antidepressants? Aren't you just substituting one addiction for another?" ...

4. "Why did you start using?" ...

5. "What was [the] rock bottom [moment during your addiction]?" ...

6. "You just need to control your habit. I can use drugs and stop whenever I want to." ...

7. "You poor thing!" ...

1. Courtney Lopresti, "10 Things to Never Say to a Recovering Addict," Sovereign Health, accessed November 19, 2017, www.sovhealth.com/alcohol-abuse/10-things-never-say-recovering-addict/.

8. *"I can't believe you used drugs. Everyone knows they're dangerous."* ...

9. *"You can still drink though, right? You were a heroin addict, not an alcoholic."* ...

10. *"Once an addict, always an addict. It's only a matter of time before you relapse."*[1]

The best thing to say to a recovering addict is to let them know they are still loved and accepted and to be understanding of the suffering they have been through. Their needs should also be accommodated—for example, a person recovering from an alcohol addiction may not want to eat at a restaurant with a bar. However, each person is different, and the key is to listen to them and what they need—they may want to just sit quietly and watch TV with a good friend, or they may need to talk. Being conscious of things that are said, being understanding, and listening are ways to start eliminating the stigma of substance-use disorders.

Drug addiction is a stigmatized disorder, and the best approach is to listen and be supportive of others as they recover from a substance-use disorder.

Andy Reid, shown here, was asked by the media to talk about his sons' drug abuse problems. He chose instead to protect their privacy until after they were officially sentenced by the court.

publicly discuss the addictions of his two sons. He refused, seeking to maintain his family's privacy. At one point during the year, Reid took a leave of absence from the team so he could devote himself full time to his family. Finally, after Britt and Garrett were sentenced, Reid and his wife, Tammy, gave an interview to a magazine reporter. The Reids acknowledged that their sons had gotten into drugs years before and that they found themselves powerless to help them break their addictions. "You have no idea, as parents you have no idea what's right and what's wrong, what's going to work and what's not going to work," Tammy Reid said. "And so you take a stab at it, you talk to psychologists and psychiatrists and friends who have been through it, anybody, to come up with a solution, what you think is best, and it doesn't always work."[33] While Britt was able to overcome his addiction and went on to work alongside his father as a coach, Garrett Reid was not so lucky; he died of a heroin overdose in August 2012.

The Economic Burden of Drug Abuse

According to a 2016 report by the U.S. Surgeon General, drug and alcohol abuse places an annual burden of $442 billion on the economy. According to the report,

> Alcohol and drug misuse and related disorders are major public health challenges that are taking an enormous toll on individuals, families, and society ... Neighborhoods and communities as a whole are also suffering as a result of alcohol- and drug-related crime and violence, abuse and neglect of children, and the increased costs of health care associated with substance misuse.[34]

This $442 billion figure accounts for health care expenses, criminal justice costs, law enforcement, and lost productivity. Lost productivity "[represents] work in the labor market and in household production that was never performed, but could reasonably be expected to be performed [without] the impact of drug abuse."[35]

There is no question that drug use negatively affects the user in the workplace. According to a study published in 2017 on the finance website MarketWatch, "Workers with substance use disorders miss nearly 50% more days [of work] than their peers, and up to six weeks of work annually."[36] In addition, 75 percent of adults with substance-use disorders are employed, and "the cost of untreated substance abuse ranges from $2,600 per employee in agriculture to more than $13,000 per employee in the information and communications sector."[37] Also, when it comes to the unemployment rate, people with substance-use disorders are more likely to be unemployed than those who do not have a substance-use disorder.

Many employers are on the lookout for workers who may be abusing drugs as well as other substances—but not necessarily to fire them. Many companies provide substance abuse programs that make counseling and rehabilitation available to workers so they can be healthy and productive again. Even though a company may have a trained specialist come in to try to provide drug intervention to employees who have an addiction, drug abuse in the workplace continues to cost the economy billions of dollars each year, although many

Steroids in Baseball

Even though Major League Baseball (MLB) instituted a drug-testing program in 2003, rumors of use of performance-enhancing drugs in baseball persisted, particularly after a 2005 book in which former baseball player Jose Canseco charged that use of steroids and human growth hormone (HGH) is widespread in the sport.

In 2006, MLB officials retained George Mitchell, a former U.S. senator, to investigate use of performance-enhancing drugs by players. Mitchell released his 409-page report in December 2007, naming 86 players—including some of the sport's biggest stars—as users of steroids and HGH. After the release of the report, officials pledged to institute stricter testing procedures and clean up the sport. As for the players named in the report, Mitchell did not recommend punishment. It soon became clear, however, that many of the stars would be made to pay a steep price, such as banishment from the Baseball Hall of Fame. According to the Mitchell report, "The illegal use of performance-enhancing substances poses a serious threat to the integrity of the game. Widespread use by players of such substances unfairly disadvantages the honest athletes who refuse to use them and raises questions about the validity of baseball records."[1]

Jose Canseco, shown here, was part of a U.S. House hearing on steroids in baseball in 2005.

1. Quoted in Jose Canseco, *Vindicated: Big Names, Big Liars, and the Battle to Save Baseball*. New York, NY: Simon Spotlight Entertainment, 2008, p. 124.

employers require prospective employees to submit to drug tests as a condition for employment. Typically, job applicants are asked to provide urine samples, which are then analyzed by drug-testing laboratories. In most cases, though, once the employees start work, they are no longer required to submit to additional drug tests.

MISUNDERSTANDING SUBSTANCE-USE DISORDERS

"Most Americans know someone with a substance use disorder, and many know someone who has lost or nearly lost a family member as a consequence of substance misuse … Yet, at the same time, few other medical conditions are surrounded by as much shame and misunderstanding as substance use disorders."

–U.S Department of Health and Human Services, *The Surgeon General's Report on Alcohol, Drugs, and Health*

Quoted in Jeff Nesbit, "The Staggering Costs, Monetary and Otherwise, of Substance Abuse," *U.S. News & World Report*, December 19, 2016. www.usnews.com/news/at-the-edge/articles/2016-12-19/drug-and-alcohol-abuse-cost-taxpayers-442b-annually-new-surgeon-generals-report-finds.

Health Care Costs

The abuse of illicit drugs and alcohol frequently leads to long-term health consequences. Drug abusers who use unclean or shared needles may spread such diseases as hepatitis and HIV; their care is often long and expensive. Additionally, innocent people are often affected by people who use drugs. They may be the victims of car crashes caused by drivers who are under the influence of drugs, for example. As these various costs rise, so does the cost of health insurance, which pays most of the medical bills in the American economy. That means the cost of health insurance continues to rise, which impacts companies and their workers, who typically share in the cost of health insurance, as well as individuals who may pay for insurance on their own.

There are many other costs as well, including the cost of investigating, prosecuting, and imprisoning drug dealers as well as the cost of running treatment and rehabilitation centers. "Drugs are a direct threat to the economic security of the United States," said John P. Walters, former director of the White House Office of National Drug Control Policy. "Drug use results in lower productivity, more workplace accidents, and higher health care costs ... When we talk about the toll that drugs take on our country—especially on our young people—we usually point to the human costs: lives ruined, potential extinguished, and dreams derailed."[38]

Research-Based Prevention

During the teenage years, normal aspects of development, such as wanting to try new things and take risks, may also mean experimenting with illicit substances. However, the brains of young adults are still developing, which makes drug use especially dangerous during this time. In addition, early use of drugs increases the chance of developing an addiction later. While some drug programs have been proven to not work very well, NIDA recommends research-based programs for young adults to prevent future drug addiction.

Unlike other programs that focus on ways to say no to drugs, these programs address certain groups depending on the program and do not merely focus on how the individual can refuse drugs. These programs are designed around current scientific evidence and are thoroughly tested. In addition, these programs are not developed around a "one size fits all" approach where the exact same program is taught to each class across the country. The broad range of available programs has been proven to reduce early use of drugs, alcohol, and tobacco. The programs "work to boost protective factors and eliminate or reduce risk factors for drug use."[39] Additionally, these programs are adjusted for different ages and can be used in various settings, such as at school or home, so the program can be taken in a group or individual setting.

The three types of programs include the following:

- *Universal programs address risk and protective factors common to all children in a given setting, such as a school or community.*

- *Selective programs target groups of children and teens who have factors that put them at increased risk of drug use.*

- *Indicated programs are designed for youth who have already begun using drugs.*[40]

While programs such as these are helpful, the United States has a history of fighting the war on drugs with laws rather than social and educational programs, and different legislation has been passed throughout the years to help combat drug use. Meanwhile, cartels and dealers continue to find new ways to get drugs in the hands of users.

CHAPTER 4

Drug Trafficking and Legislation

Drugs do not simply appear on the streets, and for the most part, they are not created in someone's home. As long as people are using drugs, no matter the amount or the frequency, there are many more people who are making a lot of money from them. It all begins with large, powerful, and violent drug cartels in places such as Afghanistan, Mexico, and Colombia. The drug is created and shipped through various channels, in a variety of creative ways, to get it into the hands of the people who are demanding it. While a large number of shipments are caught by the DEA or border patrol agents, they still are not catching it all, and traffickers simply come up with different ways to transport drugs, such as in stuffed animals, limes, or hidden under a crate of soda bottles. For as long as drug traffickers have been transporting drugs into the United States, the United States has been fighting what President Richard Nixon called a war on drugs in June 1971.

The Drug Enforcement Administration

The DEA was created in July 1973 as part of Nixon's war on drugs. The DEA works with various agencies to control the spread and production of illicit drugs. A large part of what it does involves international drug trafficking organizations whose product is destined for the United States. In addition, the DEA, in collaboration with the FDA, determines which drug gets placed into which schedule. The DEA drug schedules are as follows:

Schedule I drugs, substances, or chemicals are defined as drugs with no currently accepted medical use and a high potential for abuse ...

Schedule II drugs, substances, or chemicals are defined as drugs with a high potential for abuse, with use potentially leading to severe psychological or physical dependence. These drugs are also considered dangerous ...

Schedule III drugs, substances, or chemicals are defined as drugs with a moderate to low potential for physical and psychological dependence. Schedule III drugs abuse potential is less than Schedule I and Schedule II drugs but more than Schedule IV ...

Schedule IV drugs, substances, or chemicals are defined as drugs with a low potential for abuse and low risk of dependence ...

Schedule V drugs, substances, or chemicals are defined as drugs with lower potential for abuse than Schedule IV and consist of preparations containing limited quantities of certain narcotics. Schedule V drugs are generally used for antidiarrheal, antitussive, and analgesic purposes.[41]

The DEA confiscates illegal drugs when it finds them. Shown in this photo from 1978 are three DEA officers looking at packages of heroin that were seized at an airport in Denver, Colorado.

Schedule I drugs include heroin, LSD, ecstasy, and marijuana; Schedule II drugs include cocaine, meth, and oxycodone (OxyContin); Schedule III drugs include ketamine and steroids; Schedule IV includes prescription pills such as Ambien (a sleep aid) and Xanax (which is used to treat anxiety and panic disorders); and Schedule V includes cough syrup that contains the opioid pain medication codeine.

The DEA regularly reports its achievements when it breaks up major narcotics rings. In 2007, for example, the DEA busted a Mexico-based ring at the end of a 20-month investigation. The result of the seizure was 9,512 pounds (4,314.5 kg) of cocaine, $45.2 million in U.S. currency, 705 pounds (319.8 kg) of meth, 11 pounds (5 kg) of heroin, and 27,229 pounds (12,350.9 kg) of marijuana. DEA agents arrested more than 400 people nationwide who were alleged to have been distributing cocaine and marijuana smuggled into the United States by a single Mexican drug lord, Victor Emilio Cazares-Gastellum.

In October 2016, Afghanistan's heroin trafficking organization was disrupted by a collaboration between the U.S. DEA, U.S. Special Forces, and Afghan government officials. The seizure resulted in 20 tons (18 mt) being taken, which investigators believed was the largest seizure of heroin to date in Afghanistan, and possibly in the world. According to DEA spokesman Steven Ball,

> a conservative estimated street value was about $60 million for the 12.5 tons of morphine base, 6.4 tons of heroin base, 134 kilograms of opium, 129 kilograms of crystal heroin and 12 kilograms of hashish … After a brief gunfight with insurgents near the compound outside a remote village, the teams also found tons of chemicals in what one report called a "superlab" used to process the poppy into heroin base. The superlab was apparently a first of its kind seen by DEA agents in Afghanistan, who described the facility as "complex, sophisticated and well fortified."[42]

Indeed, the statistics compiled by law enforcement agencies are staggering. According to the U.S. Department of Justice, more than 14 million people were arrested for drug abuse violations in 2007. In 2017, according to the Federal Bureau of Prisons, more than 80,000 Americans were in prison for drug-related offenses.

Shown here are various weapons, drugs—including cocaine and crack—and other chemicals seized by the DEA in 1986 in New York City.

NOT A MORAL ISSUE

"We should be saying enough is enough. It's time we recognize as a nation that for too long, we have had a quiet epidemic on our hands. Plain and simple, drug and alcohol addiction is a disease, not a moral failing—and we must treat it as such."

–Hillary Clinton, former senator, secretary of state, and 2016 presidential candidate

Quoted in Jason M. Breslow, "How Would the Candidates Fix the Heroin Epidemic?," PBS Frontline, February 23, 2016. www.pbs.org/wgbh/frontline/article/how-would-the-candidates-fix-the-heroin-epidemic/.

War on Drugs

Although America's war on drugs can be traced back to the appointment of Harry Anslinger as head of the Federal Bureau of Narcotics in 1930, there were few resources and little organization devoted to the effort until 1968, when President Lyndon B. Johnson consolidated a number of federal law enforcement agencies into the Bureau of Narcotics and Dangerous Drugs in the U.S. Justice Department. In 1970, Congress passed the landmark U.S. Controlled Substances Act, which defined five classes of drugs according to their potential for abuse as well as their use for legitimate medicinal purposes. Since then, state governments have based their laws regulating drug use and setting penalties for possession and distribution of drugs based on the schedules of drugs established in 1970. (Over the years, other drugs have been added to the list of controlled substances.)

By then, a number of scientific studies had been issued chronicling the dangers of addiction and linking drug abuse with crime. Nixon declared drug abuse "public enemy number one in the United States"[43] and ordered a number of measures to crack down on traffickers. Some of the measures implemented during the Nixon administration, such as Operation Intercept, were quickly discarded. Under Operation Intercept, U.S. customs agents attempted to search every vehicle entering the United States along the U.S.–Mexico border. It was supposed to take just three minutes to search each vehicle, but after two weeks, the program was shelved because Operation Intercept caused huge backups at the border, causing people to wait hours before they could cross into the United States. In the meantime, the economies of the border states suffered because Mexican laborers refused to cross into the United States to come to work. Other commerce suffered as well. Operation Intercept did temporarily slow the flow of marijuana into the country, but drug abuse experts noticed that users turned to other, more readily available substances, particularly LSD, until the supply of marijuana returned to pre–Operation Intercept levels.

Lyndon B. Johnson, shown here, created the Bureau of Narcotics and Dangerous Drugs by consolidating a number of law enforcement agencies.

DISCRIMINATION AGAINST ADDICTS

"People are so discriminating when it comes to addicts. I am a good mum. Some of the people that I have seen use are people you would never think use. It's not like every drug addict is a junkie. They're people, and they're just wound up in this battle in their brain."

—Amanda, a recovering heroin and prescription pain pill addict

Quoted in Fault Lines, "Drug Aubse: 'I Watched My Babies Go Through Withdrawal,'" Aljazeera, October 28, 2017. www.aljazeera.com/indepth/features/2017/10/drug-abuse-watched-babies-withdrawal-171025083811617.html.

Other plans during the Nixon administration, such as establishment of the DEA in 1973, have been much more effective. The DEA was formed with the intention of making the war on drugs an international effort. To create the organization, agents were drawn from the Bureau of Narcotics and Dangerous Drugs as well as the U.S. Customs Service and Central Intelligence Agency (CIA). The addition of the customs and CIA agents into the DEA indicated a willingness by federal officials to root out traffickers in Latin America, Asia, and other places that served as the sources of the drugs imported into America.

Cartels in Colombia

The DEA had good reason to turn its attention to Latin American countries. It was becoming more and more obvious that Colombia and other countries in South and Central America were serving as prime exporting centers for illegal drugs. In the remote mountains of Colombia, farmers grew coca virtually untouched by police. Meanwhile, secret labs hidden deep in the Colombian jungles processed the coca into cocaine. It was all being produced under the guidance of illegal drug cartels, and there was no question that the cartels were cruel and violent.

In 1975, police seized 1,300 pounds (600 kg) of cocaine from a small airplane at the airport in Cali, Colombia. A few days later, 40 people were found murdered in the nearby city of

The French Connection

The first big victory scored by police in the drug war occurred in 1962, when police in New York City broke up what was known as the French Connection—the importation of massive amounts of heroin to the United States from France. For decades, opium grown in Turkey was ferried to Marseilles, a Mediterranean seaport city in France, where underworld traffickers converted it to heroin. From Marseilles, the heroin was shipped to America, mostly by hiding it in legitimate cargo aboard ships.

The case was cracked by two New York City detectives, Eddie Egan and Sonny Grasso, whose investigation led them to suspect a French television star, Jacques Angelvin, of smuggling heroin in a car he had transported to America aboard a ship. After searching the car, Egan and Grasso found a secret compartment containing more than 100 pounds (45 kg) of pure heroin. The drugs had a street value at the time of more than $25 million. Finding the drugs in Angelvin's car helped Egan and Grasso build a case against four other suspects, eventually leading them to a New York City home where they found another 88 pounds (40 kg) of heroin ready for distribution to street dealers.

Jacques Angelvin (right) was arrested after he was caught trying to smuggle more than 100 pounds (45 kg) of heroin into the United States.

Medellín. Investigators speculated they were low-level members of the ring who paid the ultimate price for letting the drugs fall into the hands of the police.

Carlos Lehder, shown here, bought an island close to the United States and shipped numerous cargoes of cocaine into America.

By the 1980s, the Colombian drug cartels had grown increasingly bold. They no longer carried out the pretense of operating in secret. Some of the drug kingpins built mansions, employed private armies, and were clearly operating with the knowledge of government officials and police who were on their payrolls. One Colombian kingpin, Carlos Lehder, bought most of the tiny island of Norman's Cay in the Bahamas, just 200 miles (322 km) from Florida. From the island, Lehder openly dispatched small planes to America, where they landed on remote airstrips and unloaded their cargoes of cocaine. In 1982, under pressure from the U.S. government, authorities in the Bahamas closed down the operation and kicked Lehder off the island.

Back in Colombia, American officials pressured the government to arrest cartel leaders and extradite them to the United States, where they had been indicted on drug charges. After several reformers in Colombia were assassinated by the cartels, Colombian police mounted an offensive against the drug

Dead Fish and Prosthetic Limbs: How Drugs Are Transported

Drug cartels will use virtually anything to get drugs into the United States. Whether it is miles of tunnels under the U.S.–Mexico border, a plane, or a submarine, they will go to any lengths to get their product to its final destination. Additionally, with a multi-million dollar industry, they have the means to get as creative, complex, and expensive as they want.

Illicit drugs have been concealed inside prosthetic limbs and attached to the insides of book covers, and there have even been luggage wheels made of heroin. Cocaine has been hidden in lollipops and other candy, in cans of beans, among dead fish, and in meat containers before being frozen. It has even been molded to fit the shape of someone's skull so it could be hidden under a wig. Meth, meanwhile, has been packed into pineapples.

In 2015, Mexican soldiers found what appeared to be powdered doughnuts, but the doughnuts were found to be sprinkled with cocaine instead of powdered sugar.

A man was arrested in Florida after he was discovered with this Cookie Monster doll, which was filled with cocaine.

While it might seem like mechanical drones are a good idea for transporting drugs, in reality, they are not. Drug traffickers transport thousands of pounds of product, and drones only allow for a few pounds at most. Instead, this technology would be more likely to be used for surveillance to spy on border agents.

kingpins, killing some in violent clashes and jailing others. In 1993, one of the top Colombian drug kingpins, Pablo Escobar, was killed in a shootout with Colombian police.

Meanwhile, efforts in other Latin American countries were also starting to show results. In 1988, U.S. prosecutors indicted Panamanian president Manuel Noriega, accused of laundering drug money and providing Colombian kingpins with safe havens in his country, where they had established laboratories. A year later, American troops invaded Panama, where they captured Noriega and brought him back to Florida. Noriega was tried, convicted, and sentenced to 40 years in prison. Federal authorities have continued to target countries in Central and South America. In 2000, President Bill Clinton launched Plan Colombia, a program to fund Colombian military initiatives against drug kingpins. Initially budgeted at $1 billion, Plan Colombia has grown into a more than $10 billion initiative that continues to be funded each year by Congress.

While it would seem that the initiatives against the Colombian cartels, the arrests of high-level traffickers such as Noriega, and the implementation of programs such as Plan Colombia would have virtually wiped out the Latin American drug trade, that has not been the case. Despite all those efforts, drugs continue to flow into the United States.

Drug-Related Violence

Unfortunately, while the effects of drugs are tragic enough, there is also violence involved, whether in small towns or cities or through direct action of a large drug cartel. In many cases, drug violence can be particularly horrific. In the early morning hours of June 17, 2006, police in New Orleans, Louisiana, were called to Josephine Street in the Central City neighborhood. When they arrived, police were stunned by what they found: the bodies of five teenagers, all killed by gunfire. Later that day, police arrested 19-year-old Michael Anderson and charged him with the murders of the five young people, who were all between the ages of 16 and 19. According to police, the five victims were sitting in a car when Anderson approached the vehicle, killing the driver first and then opening fire into the car, spraying the interior of the vehicle with 20 bullets. Police speculated that Anderson killed the youths in a dispute over drug territory. In 2016, a new indictment accused a man named Telly Hankton of the murders. His reasoning behind them was to maintain his role as leading gun supplier for his area. However, Anderson remained in jail due to a life sentence for pleading guilty to running a drug ring, among other crimes.

Antidrug Laws and Programs

Congress has responded to these drug abuse trends by making drug enforcement a national priority. In 2008, Congress appropriated, or set aside, more than $2 billion for the budget of the DEA. In addition, state and local governments also spend hundreds of millions of dollars on drug enforcement activities. The money helps outfit local police with electronic surveillance equipment, provides overtime pay to police officers for manning stakeouts and to undercover officers working on round-the-clock cases, pays street money to informants, and provides cash for numerous other details involved in putting together drug cases.

Indeed, Congress and the state legislatures are continually looking for ways to strengthen the laws against drug dealing. For example, in 1986, prompted by the death of Len Bias, a basketball star who died of a cocaine overdose, Congress passed the Anti-Drug Abuse Act, setting mandatory-minimum sentences for people convicted of dealing and possessing drugs. This means drug dealers must be sentenced to a minimum amount of time in jail; the exact amount of time varies. For instance, the second time someone is caught with marijuana, they must stay in jail for no less than 15 days no matter what amount they had in their possession, even if they were not intending to sell it. In passing the law, Congress also appropriated huge sums of money for additional antidrug law enforcement measures, including $97 million to build new prisons. Other measures adopted by the federal government include the 1998 Brownsville Agreement, in which American and Mexican authorities agreed to share intelligence about drug activities on both sides of the border, and the Plan Colombia program. In 2007, President George W. Bush proposed a new antidrug program aimed at helping Mexico root out traffickers. The program would provide Mexican authorities with hundreds of millions of dollars to aid police. The United States has also offered military equipment, including helicopters, to assist in the program.

At the time Bush proposed the plan, Mexico was in the middle of a long-running turf war among traffickers that had taken the lives of around 3,000 people, most of them low-level criminals. Henry Cuellar, a congressman from Texas, said he would support the initial investment of hundreds of millions of dollars into the plan, with the understanding that the program's budget could eventually grow into the billions—as it has for Plan Colombia.

Opposition to the Drug War

While law enforcement authorities concentrate their efforts on stemming the flow of drugs over the Mexican border, traffickers have found ways to bring their drugs across the Canadian border. Whenever authorities think of a way to decrease the drug trade, the traffickers come up with new ways to avoid the police. Many critics compare the billions spent on enforcement with the success of drug dealers and wonder whether it is worth it.

Critics of the drug war suggest that the money the government pours into Plan Colombia and similar international efforts can be better spent in America on intervention programs to convince young people to avoid drugs as well as rehabilitation programs to help former users stay clean. According to a *Rolling Stone* analysis in 2011, 63 percent of all the money spent on the drug war by the United States—around $8.4 billion per year at that time—was spent on law enforcement either in America or in other countries. The rest of the money, about $4.8 billion, was spent on treatment programs for drug abusers as well as drug prevention programs. One believer in shifting focus from law enforcement to prevention and rehabilitation is Lee Brown, the former head of the White House Office of National Drug Control Policy. Brown said, "I saw how little we were doing to help addicts, and I thought, 'This is crazy … This is how we should be breaking the cycle of addiction and crime, and we're just doing nothing.'"[44]

Moreover, opponents of the drug war believe that most people arrested in the United States are not major traffickers but rather small-time dealers or individual users. "Taxpayers spend between $7.5 and $10 billion annually arresting and prosecuting individuals for marijuana violations," said Allen St. Pierre, former executive director of NORML (formerly the National Organization for the Reform of Marijuana Laws). "Almost 90 percent of these arrests are for marijuana possession only. This is a clear misapplication of the criminal sanction and a tremendous waste of fiscal resources."[45]

Opponents of the drug war have not been able to convince many political leaders of the idea that it is foolish to continue spending billions of dollars each year on rounding up drug traffickers, prosecuting them, and throwing them in jail. In America, no politician wants to be accused of not doing enough to solve crime; many fear that leaving drug dealers alone will make it seem as though they do not take the problems of addiction and the drug trade seriously.

CHAPTER 5

The Legalization Debate

One of the most controversial views on drugs is the possible legalization of them. This side of the drug abuse debate comes with many questions, including whether all drugs should be legalized. If not, then which ones should be legalized? Will the legalization of drugs create more problems than it solves? In addition, some people who originally believed all drugs should be legalized changed their opinions after the heroin epidemic, proving that this debate has no clear answers. A good solution may not be found for years, if ever.

What Would Legalization Allow?

Given the overwhelming cost of the drug war as well as the limited results that have been produced over the years, some people argue that drugs should be legalized. Legalization would allow the government to control distribution, ensure the safety and purity of the substances, and even generate tax revenue from their use. Others oppose outright legalization but suggest that criminal laws are too harsh on individual users and that some forms of drug use should be decriminalized, meaning penalties would be reduced or eliminated.

A poll commissioned in 2002 by NORML found that 61 percent of Americans oppose arresting and jailing marijuana users. Another poll published in 2017 by Gallup, an organization that analyzes data, showed that 64 percent of Americans believe in full legalization of marijuana. Indeed, many people equate the laws against drugs with the 18th Amendment to the U.S. Constitution, the largely unsuccessful law that prohibited the manufacture and sale of alcohol.

Meanwhile, many people also favor the legalization of marijuana for medicinal purposes. As of early 2018, 29 states and Washington, D.C., have legalized marijuana for medicinal purposes. Many people who suffer from cancer, AIDS, and other painful diseases and conditions use marijuana as a painkiller or to stimulate their appetite so they can eat.

"For me, marijuana eases the pain in my feet—on a scale of 1 to 10, it brings it from a 6 down to a 4 and keeps it there," said former television talk show host Montel Williams, who suffers from multiple sclerosis, a painful nerve disease. "[Marijuana] makes it manageable so I can deal with the rest of my day … Why should it not be available?"[46]

As of 2018, 29 states and Washington, D.C., have legalized marijuana, shown here, for medical purposes.

A CANCER PATIENT'S VIEW

"I shouldn't be considered a criminal to have my choice. As long as I'm not harming others, I should be able to do it."

–Bill Bohns, a cancer patient from Salem, Massachusetts, who supports the use of medicinal marijuana

Quoted in Taryn Plumb, "Changes Sought in Marijuana Laws, but Police Warn That Marijuana Use Isn't Harmless," *Boston Globe*, February 10, 2008. www.boston.com/news/local/articles/2008/02/10/changes_sought_in_marijuana_laws.

Drug Policies Around the World

Most advocates for legalizing drugs point to the success of the Netherlands as well as other European countries that have either legalized marijuana or have all but eliminated penalties for individuals. They insist that crime rates have dropped in those countries. In the Dutch city of Amsterdam, an adult can walk into a coffeehouse and buy a brownie with marijuana baked into it without breaking the law. It is illegal to smoke or eat pot, or marijuana, outdoors in Amsterdam. However, the city's police are known to be rather tolerant, and few people are arrested.

According to former New Mexico governor Gary Johnson, who has called for the decriminalization of drugs,

> Holland is the only country in the world that has a rational drug policy. I had always heard that Holland, where marijuana is decriminalized and controlled, had out-of-control drug abuse and crime. But when I researched it, I learned that's untrue. It's propaganda. Holland has 60 percent of the drug use—both hard drugs and marijuana—that the United States has. They have a quarter of the crime rate, a quarter of the homicide rate, a quarter the violent crime rate, and a tenth the incarceration rate.[47]

In many foreign nations, particularly in Europe, countries have assessed the dangers of marijuana and have responded with a wide variety of laws. Indeed, what is legal in one country may be illegal in another. For example, marijuana use in Belgium is illegal. However, in the Czech Republic, it is permissible to possess a small amount of marijuana for personal use, but dealers are prosecuted.

Some countries do not regard possession of a small amount of marijuana as a crime, but they still want to punish users. Therefore, they have passed "administrative sanctions" on people caught in possession of pot. Administrative sanctions may include suspension of a driver's license or the requirement for the user to report to police headquarters every day. Among the European nations that use administrative sanctions are Croatia, Italy, Portugal, and Spain. Author Brian Preston, whose book *Pot Planet: Adventures in Global Marijuana Culture* examines international drug laws, explained that "Spanish legal tradition is non-intrusive. It gives great respect to an individual's right to privacy, which makes the state reluctant to prosecute people who are growing a few plants for personal consumption."[48]

In most European countries, the lenient laws apply only to marijuana use. Abusers of harder drugs such as cocaine, heroin, and ecstasy typically face criminal prosecution and stiff penalties.

While European countries are lenient with their laws on marijuana, hard drugs such as heroin (shown here) come with stiffer penalties and criminal prosecution.

Harm Reduction

Harm reduction involves strategies aimed at reducing the stigma, or negative views, and negative consequences associated with substance use. The movement involves respect and social justice for the rights of people who are using drugs. Harm reduction incorporates a variety of strategies, including management of drug use, safer use of drugs, abstinence from drug use, and more. These strategies are based on the individual's and community's needs rather than a universal approach or formula. The Harm Reduction Coalition adheres to the following principles of harm reduction practice:

- *Accepts, for better and or worse, that licit and illicit drug use is part of our world and chooses to work to minimize its harmful effects rather than simply ignore or condemn them.*

- *Understands drug use as a complex, multi-faceted phenomenon that encompasses a continuum of behaviors from severe abuse to total abstinence, and acknowledges that some ways of using drugs are clearly safer than others.*

- *Establishes quality of individual and community life and well-being—not necessarily cessation of all drug use—as the criteria for successful interventions and policies.*

- *Calls for the non-judgmental, non-coercive provision of services and resources to people who use drugs and the communities in which they live in order to assist them in reducing attendant harm.*

- *Ensures that drug users and those with a history of drug use routinely have a real voice in the creation of programs and policies designed to serve them.*

- *Affirms drugs users themselves as the primary agents of reducing the harms of their drug use, and seeks to empower users to share information and support each other in strategies which meet their actual conditions of use.*

- *Recognizes that the realities of poverty, class, racism, social isolation, past trauma, sex-based discrimination and other social inequalities affect both people's vulnerability to and capacity for effectively dealing with drug-related harm.*

- *Does not attempt to minimize or ignore the real and tragic harm and danger associated with licit and illicit drug use.*[1]

1. "Principles of Harm Reduction," Harm Reduction Coalition, accessed November 26, 2017. harmreduction.org/about-us/principles-of-harm-reduction/.

State Laws versus Federal Laws

In America, federal laws prohibit illicit drug use, but they are largely aimed at big-time traffickers. Typically, the DEA does not concern itself with arresting people for possession of small quantities. However, all state governments have enacted laws regarding the possession, manufacture, and sale of illicit drugs. Some are quite strict, but others are lenient—at least when they apply to possession. For example, in Kentucky, possession of less than 8 ounces (226.8 g) of marijuana is a 45-day prison sentence. However, this same amount with the intent to distribute can carry a one-year prison sentence. In Maryland, possession of 0.35 ounce (10 g) does not carry a prison sentence. With harder drugs, though, penalties are typically stiffer and judges less lenient, particularly for people caught selling drugs.

Many state legislatures continually study their drug laws and question whether they are appropriate. Some states have decriminalized drugs, making possession of a small amount of marijuana a civil offense. This means defendants are not prosecuted in criminal court, although they may have to pay small fines if found in violation of the state's narcotics laws.

Federal laws vary depending on amounts, the type of drug, and the offense. For example, 2,204.6 pounds (1,000 kg) of marijuana carries a prison sentence of at least 10 years for the first offense and at least 20 years for the second offense. For 3.5 ounces to 35 ounces (100 to 999 g) of heroin, the first offense is at least 5 years and no more than 40 years, while the second offense is at least 10 years and not more than a life sentence.

Full Legalization of Marijuana

The movement to decriminalize marijuana may be gaining support largely because pot has become so common in American society. According to a 2017 poll by the Marist College Institute for Public Opinion, 52 percent of Americans over the age of 18 have tried marijuana at least once. In many places, people have become much more open about using the drug.

Vending Machines for Marijuana

Vending machines used to be for snacks and sodas, but they can now dispense things from cosmetics to head-phones—and some even dispense marijuana. The company American Green revealed a prototype in 2017 that used biometric verification technology to sell age-restricted and controlled items such as marijuana and alcohol. These vend-ing machines are able to screen potential buyers by having the customer create an account with a government-issued ID and doctor's prescription if needed (such as for medical marijuana). The machine also scans a fingerprint and takes a picture to ensure the correct person is making the purchase.

These machines are ideal for customers who do not want to make a face-to-face transaction or do not have time to wait in a dispensary. In addition, they are ideal for senior citizen centers who want marijuana or need it for a medical condition but are not able to drive to a dispensary to get it.

Marijuana vending machines such as these are ideal for customers who do not have time to wait at dispensaries or do not want to make a face-to-face transaction.

Howard Finkelstein, a lawyer from Broward County, Florida, said that people who obtain marijuana for their personal use are not criminals—they are simply people who want to engage in an activity that affects no one but themselves. "We're making war on our own people," Finkelstein insisted. "We take good fathers and lawyers and doctors and wives and make them outlaws."[49]

Allen St. Pierre has called for Congress and the state legislatures to take a much different approach to marijuana. Instead of regarding pot as an illegal drug, or even decriminalizing the use of marijuana, St. Pierre believes the government should legalize the drug and enact standards that would regulate its growth and distribution. St. Pierre also suggests that the government could charge heavy taxes on its use, much the way the federal and state governments tax the sale of alcohol and tobacco products. According to St. Pierre,

> It makes no sense to continue to treat nearly half of all Americans as criminals for their use of a substance that poses no greater—and arguably far fewer—health risks than alcohol or tobacco. A better and more sensible solution would be to tax and regulate cannabis in a manner similar to alcohol and tobacco.[50]

Additionally, many people believe there is a racist component to the current marijuana laws. According to the *Huffington Post*, when Harry Anslinger first outlawed marijuana, he did it partially because he did not like the fact that many of the people using the drug were people of color; he expressed the racist belief that it made them feel they were "as good as white men."[51] Today, although these kind of statements are no longer made by most politicians and federal officials, the enforcement of anti-marijuana laws continues to disproportionately affect people of color: White people who are caught with marijuana are often let off with a warning or a small fine; people of color face much stricter consequences. A 2013 study by the American Civil Liberties Union (ACLU) found that "blacks across the nation were nearly four times more likely than whites to be arrested on charges of marijuana possession in 2010, despite data that suggested they use the drug at about the same rate."[52] Other studies have found similar results.

WHO IS THE ENEMY?

"In declaring war on drugs, we've declared war on our fellow citizens. War requires 'hostiles'—enemies we can demonize, fear and loathe. This unfortunate categorization of millions of our citizens justifies treating them as dope fiends, less than human."

—Norm Stamper, former police chief of Seattle, Washington

Norm Stamper, "Legalize Drugs–All of Them," *Seattle Times*, December 4, 2005. seattletimes. nwsource.com/html/opinion/2002661006_sunstamper04.html.

Medicinal Marijuana

While the debate continues over decriminalization of marijuana for recreational use, there is plenty of support for legalizing marijuana for medicinal use. For years, people who suffer from cancer and other painful diseases have called on the states as well as the federal government to allow them to use marijuana to ease their symptoms. In addition to providing pain relief, proponents of medicinal marijuana also insist that the drug makes them feel better about themselves and helps relieve depression over their physical ailments. Also, proponents suggest, marijuana's tendency to make users hungry can help restore strength in people whose illnesses make them lose their appetites. They suggest that AIDS patients could greatly benefit from marijuana use since AIDS often drains patients of their strength. By eating better and maintaining their strength, they argue, AIDS patients can better fight the disease.

The use of marijuana for medicinal purposes actually has a very long history. When Congress passed the Marijuana Tax Act, pharmaceutical companies won an exemption permitting them to continue to use extract of cannabis in painkillers. At the time, around 30 medications containing marijuana extract were on the market. Eventually, those medications were phased out and were finally banned in 1970 with the adoption of the Controlled Substances Act.

However, even after those drugs dropped out of the marketplace, people in pain have continued to find relief in pot. As one man who suffered from AIDS for more than 20 years explained,

Physically, it helps with the nausea and my appetite. It's the only way I can keep food down and my medications. Plus, I'm able to focus a little better. Rather than being so anxious and depressed about my prognosis, I think about what I need to do to try and survive rather than always feel the anxiety of dying.[53]

Medicinal marijuana dispensaries such as this one are highly beneficial to people who have painful illnesses or need an appetite stimulant.

The Challenges Ahead

As of early 2018, marijuana has been legalized for medicinal purposes by 29 states and decriminalized for recreational purposes by 22 states. However, the legalization of all drugs is a debate with very strong opinions on each side. Marijuana has been shown to have medicinal benefits for people suffering from painful illnesses such as cancer or AIDS and has been proven to not be addictive. When it comes to cocaine or heroin, however, these drugs have been shown to be highly addictive with no medicinal properties, and the heroin epidemic has led to a crackdown on the amount of prescription painkillers prescribed because a large part of the heroin epidemic has stemmed from prescription painkiller addiction.

Each country has had to work out the laws it thinks work best. For instance, according to *Fortune* magazine, Portugal

> decriminalized all drugs in 2001 amid a heroin addiction crisis and soaring numbers of drug-related AIDS deaths. Possessing small amounts of illicit substances is now treated as a public health problem. Instead of facing jail time, drug users who are caught must meet with medical experts, social workers, and psychologists who assess their situation and often direct them toward treatment or other rehabilitative services.

> The results of this policy have been astonishing. Drug use has declined across all age groups. Overdose deaths have plummeted to just three per million adults, the second lowest rate in the European Union. For comparison, the drug overdose death rate in the U.S. is a staggering 185 per million adults. Portugal's drug-related HIV infections have fallen by 94% since 2001. And the number of people arrested for criminal drug offenses has declined by over 60%, which has allowed Portugal to channel money once spent on arresting and imprisoning addicts toward more effective treatment programs.[54]

One Portuguese counselor stated that since decriminalization, counselors are in a better position to help people who have an addiction, and it is cheaper to treat a drug user than to put them in jail.

However, some people are against drug legalization because of the way opioids were originally marketed. Pharmaceutical companies met with doctors and recommended them for all kinds of pain, from minor to severe, promising they were not addictive and had no negative effects. Of course, this was quickly proven false, but not before many people had suffered. According to one person who previously supported legalization of all drugs,

> *while many of these deaths are now linked to illicit drugs like heroin and fentanyl, the source of the epidemic—what got people started on a chain to harder drugs—was opioid painkillers, and legal painkillers were still linked to most opioid overdose deaths as of 2015 ... This was exactly what anti-legalization activists have warned about: Companies got a hold of a dangerous, addictive product, marketed it irresponsibly, and lobbied for lax rules. The government's regulatory response floundered. The government even worked with the drug companies in some cases—under the influence of lobbying, campaign donations, and drugmaker-funded advocacy groups. And people got addicted and died.*

> *Looking at this crisis, it slowly but surely dawned on me: Maybe full legalization isn't the right answer to the war on drugs. Maybe the US just can't handle regulating these potentially deadly substances in a legal environment. Maybe some form of prohibition—albeit a less stringent kind than what we have today—is the way to go.*[55]

These views show that the legalization debate does not have a clear answer. Until a decision is made, if one ever is, many believe the best policy is to treat each person's addiction individually instead of using a universal formula and to remove the stigma that surrounds drug abuse.

Introduction: The Tragedy of Addiction

1. Harrison Jacobs, "Where Hillary Clinton and Donald Trump Stand on the Opioid Epidemic," *Business Insider*, September 24, 2016. www.businessinsider.com/clinton-and-trump-on-opioid-drug-addiction-treatment-2016-9.

2. Jacobs, "Where Hillary Clinton and Donald Trump Stand on the Opioid Epidemic."

3. "Drugs, Brains, and Behavior: The Science of Addiction," National Institute on Drug Abuse, last updated July 2014. www.drugabuse.gov/publications/drugs-brains-behavior-science-addiction/preventing-drug-abuse-best-strategy.

4. Susan Scutti, "New Potential for Marijuana: Treating Drug Addiction," CNN, May 17, 2017. www.cnn.com/2017/05/17/health/addiction-cannabis-harm-reduction/index.html.

Chapter 1: Drug Abuse in the United States

5. Kristin Romey, "Ancient Cannabis 'Burial Shroud' Discovered in Desert Oasis," *National Geographic*, October 4, 2016. news.nationalgeographic.com/2016/10/marijuana-cannabis-pot-weed-burial-shroud-china-ancient-discovery-scythians-turpan-archaeology-botany/.

6. Quoted in Dale L. June, Mohamad Khatibloo, and Gregorio Estevane, eds., *The Re-Evolution of American Street Gangs.* Boca Raton, FL: CRC Press, 2016, p. 41.

7. Quoted in S. K. Chatterjee, *Legal Aspects of International Drug Control.* Hingham, MA: Kluwer Boston, 1981, p. 46.

8. Quoted in Larry Sloman, *Reefer Madness: The History of Marijuana in America.* New York, NY: St. Martin's Griffin, 1979, p. 81.

9. "Did You Know … Marijuana was Once a Legal Cross-Border Import?," U.S. Customs and Border Protection, October 6, 2015. www.cbp.gov/about/history/did-you-know/marijuana.

10. Robert Sabbag, *Snowblind: A Brief Career in the Cocaine Trade*. New York, NY: Vintage, 1990, p. 80.

11. Quoted in Alex Tresniowski, "Taped in the Act," *People*, October 30, 2000. people.com/archive/taped-in-the-act-vol-54-no-18/.

12. Tom Sheve, "How Meth Works," HowStuffWorks, accessed November 14, 2017. science.howstuffworks.com/meth3.htm.

13. Onell R. Soto and Leslie Berestein, "2,400-Foot Tunnel 'Beats Them All,'" *San Diego Union Tribune*, January 27, 2006. legacy.sandiegouniontribune.com/news/mexico/tijuana/20060127-9999-1n27tunnel.html.

14. Melissa Healy, "Over-the-Counter Painkillers Treated Painful Injuries Just as Well as Opioids in New Study," *Los Angeles Times*, November 7, 2017. beta.latimes.com/science/sciencenow/la-sci-sn-pain-opioids-ibuprofen-20171107-story.html.

15. Healy, "Over-the-Counter Painkillers Treated Painful Injuries Just as Well as Opioids in New Study."

Chapter 2: The Effects of Drug Use

16. Quoted in Kathy Ehrich Dowd and Stephen M. Silverman, "Heath Ledger's Death Was Accidental Overdose," *People*, February 5, 2008. www.people.com/people/article/0,,20176284,00.html.

17. Quoted in Edward M. Brecher, *Licit and Illicit Drugs*. New York, NY: Little, Brown and Company, 1972, p. 274.

18. Joseph Stromberg, "A Scientific Explanation of How Marijuana Causes the Munchies," *Smithsonian*, February 9, 2014. www.smithsonianmag.com/science-nature/scientific-explanation-how-marijuana-causes-munchies-180949660/.

19. "Drugs, Brains, and Behavior: The Science of Addiction," National Institute on Drug Abuse.

20. Olivia Gordon, *The Agony of Ecstasy*. New York, NY: Continuum, 2004, p. 68.

21. "Drugs, Brains, and Behavior: The Science of Addiction," National Institute on Drug Abuse.

22. Deborah Condon, "Heroin Causes Alzheimer-like Brain Damage," IrishHealth, June 27, 2005, www.irishhealth.com/article.html?level=4&id=7759.

23. Quoted in "Marijuana Affects Blood Vessels," BBC News, February 8, 2005. news.bbc.co.uk/1/hi/health/4244489.stm.

24. Christopher Ingraham, "Heavy Pot Use Can Permanently Damage Short-Term Memory, Study Shows," *The Seattle Times*, last updated April 25, 2016. www.seattletimes.com/nation-world/study-says-heavy-marijuana-use-can-damage-short-term-memory/.

25. Richard Marques, "Cocaine Use Can Lead to a Hole in the Roof of Your Mouth," *Independent*, August 10, 2015. www.independent.co.uk/life-style/health-and-families/features/cocaine-use-can-lead-to-a-hole-in-the-roof-of-your-mouth-10448496.html.

26. The American Cancer Society Medical and Editorial Content Team, "Small Cell Lung Cancer Risk Factors," American Cancer Society, last updated May 16, 2016. www.cancer.org/cancer/small-cell-lung-cancer/causes-risks-prevention/risk-factors.html.

27. Maggie May Ethridge, "This Is Exactly What Happens When You Overdose," Vice, June 29, 2017. tonic.vice.com/en_us/article/a3dzyb/this-is-exactly-what-happens-when-you-overdose.

Chapter 3: Societal Impact

28. "Drug Abuse and Addiction: One of America's Most Challenging Health Problems," National Institute on Drug Abuse, October 25, 1999. archives.drugabuse.gov/about/welcome/aboutdrugabuse/magnitude/.

29. Perry Stein and Lindsey Bever, "The Opioid Crisis Is Straining the Nation's Foster-Care System," *Washington Post*, July 1, 2017. www.washingtonpost.com/national/the-opioid-crisis-is-straining-the-nations-foster-care-systems/2017/06/30/97759fb2-52a1-11e7-91eb-9611861a988f_story.html?utm_term=.4676944e0af4.

30. Stein and Bever, "The Opioid Crisis Is Straining the Nation's Foster-Care System."

31. Teresa Wiltz, "Drug-Addiction Epidemic Creates Crisis in Foster Care," The Pew Charitable Trusts, October 7, 2016. www.pewtrusts.org/en/research-and-analysis/blogs/stateline/2016/10/07/drug-addiction-epidemic-creates-crisis-in-foster-care.

32. Wiltz, "Drug-Addiction Epidemic Creates Crisis in Foster Care."

33. Quoted in Karen Araiza, "Garrett Reid Struggled with Addiction for Years," NBC Philadelphia, last updated August 7, 2012. www.nbcphiladelphia.com/news/local/Garrett-Reid-Drug-History-Eagles-Coach-Andy-Reid-165059826.html.

34. Quoted in Jeff Nesbit, "The Staggering Costs, Monetary and Otherwise, of Substance Abuse," *U.S. News & World Report*, December 19, 2016. www.usnews.com/news/at-the-edge/articles/2016-12-19/drug-and-alcohol-abuse-cost-taxpayers-442b-annually-new-surgeon-generals-report-finds.

35. White House Office of National Drug Control Policy, "The Economic Costs of Drug Abuse in the United States, 1992–2002," p. x. www.whitehousedrugpolicy.gov/publications/economic_costs/.

36. Quentin Fottrell, "Americans Struggling with Opioid Addiction Miss 50% More Work than Everyone Else," MarketWatch, October 28, 2017. www.marketwatch.com/story/americas-prescription-drug-epidemic-is-a-worsening-problem-for-employers-2017-03-13.

37. Fottrell, "Americans Struggling with Opioid Addiction Miss 50% More Work than Everyone Else."

38. Quoted in "Illegal Drugs Drain $160 Billion a Year from American Economy," White House Office of National Drug Control Policy, January 23, 2002. www.whitehousedrugpolicy.gov/news/press02/012302.html.

39. "Drugs, Brains, and Behavior: The Science of Addiction," National Institute on Drug Abuse.

40. "Drugs, Brains, and Behavior: The Science of Addiction," National Institute on Drug Abuse.

Chapter 4: Drug Trafficking and Legislation

41. "Drug Schedules," DEA.gov, accessed November 21, 2017. www.dea.gov/druginfo/ds.shtml.

42. James Gordon Meek, "DEA: Heroin Haul Largest Ever in Afghanistan, 'If Not the World,'" ABC News, December 15, 2016. abcnews.go.com/International/dea-heroin-haul-largest-afghanistan-world/story?id=44216333.

43. Quoted in "Thirty Years of America's Drug War," PBS *Frontline*, accessed November 21, 2017. www.pbs.org/wgbh/pages/frontline/shows/drugs/cron.

44. Quoted in Ben Wallace-Wells, "How America Lost the War on Drugs," *Rolling Stone*, March 24, 2011. www.rollingstone.com/politics/news/how-america-lost-the-war-on-drugs-20110324.

45. Quoted in "Economists Slam War on Drugs; Cost-Effectiveness of Incarceration Doubtful, National Academy of Sciences Report Says," NORML, April 12, 2001. norml.org/index.cfm?Group_ID=4287.

Chapter 5: The Legalization Debate

46. Quoted in "Montel Williams Joins Push for New Jersey Medical Marijuana Law," *USA Today*, June 6, 2006. usatoday30.usatoday.com/life/people/2006-06-06-williams-marijuana_x.htm.

47. Quoted in Brian Preston, *Pot Planet: Adventures in Global Marijuana Culture*. New York, NY: Grove, 2002, p. 146.

48. Preston, *Pot Planet*, p. 182.

49. Quoted in Lydia Martin and Fred Tasker, "Marijuana's Double Standard Persists," *Miami Herald,* June 4, 2007.

50. Quoted in "Marijuana Arrests for the Year 2006—829,625—Tops Record High," NORML, September 24, 2007. norml.org/index.cfm?Group_ID=7370.

51. Quoted in Nick Wing, "Marijuana Prohibition Was Racist from the Start. Not Much Has Changed," *Huffington Post*, January 14, 2014. www.huffingtonpost.com/2014/01/14/marijuana-prohibition-racist_n_4590190.html.

52. Wing, "Marijuana Prohibition."

53. Quoted in David Harsanyi, "Medical-Marijuana User Taken on a Bad Trip by Legal System," *Denver Post*, March 29, 2007. www.denverpost.com/headlines/ci_5542663.

54. Jeffrey Miron, "Could Legalizing All Drugs Solve America's Opioid Epidemic?," *Fortune*, September 19, 2017. fortune.com/2017/09/19/jeff-sessions-opioid-epidemic-legalize-all-drugs/.

55. German Lopez, "I Used to Support Legalizing All Drugs. Then the Opioid Epidemic Happened," Vox, September 12, 2017. www.vox.com/policy-and-politics/2017/4/20/15328384/opioid-epidemic-drug-legalization.

Chapter 1: Drug Abuse in the United States

1. What were some of the factors that prompted Congress to adopt the U.S. Pure Food and Drug Act in 1906?

2. How have prescription painkillers led to a heroin epidemic?

3. What is a patent medicine?

Chapter 2: The Effects of Drug Use

1. What are some of the ways drugs affect neurotransmitters and receptors?

2. How does the brain react to pleasurable experiences?

3. How does drug abuse affect memory?

Chapter 3: Societal Impact

1. What are some of the ways in which drug abuse has had an economic impact on American society?

2. How is drug abuse affecting the foster care system?

3. What are some things that should not be said to people who are recovering from drug abuse? What things can you say or do instead?

Chapter 4: Drug Trafficking and Legislation

1. In 1973, the new U.S. Drug Enforcement Administration drew agents from the U.S. Customs Service and the Central Intelligence Agency. How did these agents and the new organization change the scope of the drug war?

2. What are the Drug Enforcement Administration drug schedules, and what types of drugs does each schedule include?

3. How do drug cartels in other countries get their product into the United States?

Chapter 5: The Legalization Debate

1. Do you think hard drugs, such as cocaine and heroin, should be legalized? Why or why not?

2. What are some drug policies in other parts of the world?

3. What is harm reduction?

Narconon

7065 Hollywood Boulevard
Los Angeles, CA 90028
(800) 775-8750
www.narconon.org

This organization provides plenty of information on drugs, including history, effects, and treatment. Additionally, the organization is a rehabilitation program with facilities around the world. They are available to talk 24 hours a day if a person or one of their loved ones has a drug addiction.

Narcotics Anonymous

PO Box 9999
Van Nuys, CA 91409
(818) 773-9999
fsmail@na.org
www.na.org

Established in the 1950s, Narcotics Anonymous supports thousands of groups in America and foreign countries, which hold more than 67,000 weekly meetings a year. The meetings serve as forums for members to help one another emerge from their addictions.

National Council on Alcoholism and Drug Dependence (NCADD)

217 Broadway, Suite 712
New York, NY 10007
800-622-2255
national@ncadd.org
www.ncadd.org

NCADD runs a referral hotline, and its website includes information on drugs, up-to-date news, and information for family and friends on how to help a loved one who is addicted to a substance.

National Institute on Drug Abuse (NIDA)

6001 Executive Boulevard
Room 5213
Bethesda, MD 20892
(301) 443-1124
www.nida.nih.gov

> NIDA is one of the leading organizations supporting research on drug abuse and addiction. Its website features updated scientific information and research on various drugs as well as information on treatments.

Substance Abuse and Mental Health Services Administration (SAMHSA)

5600 Fishers Lane
Rockville, MD 20857
(240) 726-4727 or (800) 662-4357 (national helpline)
www.samhsa.gov

> An agency of the U.S. Department of Health and Human Services, SAMHSA helps develop programs for people who are at risk for abusing drugs and assesses the spread of drug use in American society. SAMHSA also runs a national information and referral helpline 24 hours a day, 7 days a week, 365 days a year for individuals and families who are facing substance use disorders or mental health disorders.

Books

Ellis, Carol, and Robert Grayson. *Drug Cartels and Smugglers.*
Pittsburgh, PA: El Dorado Ink, 2013.
> This book examines cartels in Mexico, drug deals in prison,
> and more, along with how the United States is tackling
> the issue.

Goldsmith, Connie. *Addiction and Overdose: Confronting an
American Crisis.* Minneapolis, MN: Twenty-First Century
Books, 2017.
> This book examines how people become addicted to drugs
> and includes stories from people in recovery as well as
> those who have lost a loved one to drug abuse.

Newton, Michael. *Drug Enforcement Administration.* New York,
NY: Infobase Publishing, 2011.
> Newton's book details information on the Drug Enforce-
> ment Administration (DEA) and how it is fighting drug
> trafficking. The book also provides a history of the DEA
> and various drug cartels throughout a number of countries.

Parks, Peggy J. *The Dangers of Painkillers.* San Diego, CA:
ReferencePoint Press, 2017.
> This book presents an in-depth view of painkillers and
> discusses the problem, effects, treatment, and more.

Shantz-Hilkes, Chloe. *Hooked: When Addiction Hits Home.*
Toronto, ON: Annick Press, Limited, 2013.
> This book is a collection of interviews with people who
> have lived with a person who was addicted to drugs and
> details how they coped with the experience.

Websites

Drug Enforcement Administration (DEA)

www.dea.gov/index.shtml

> The DEA's website includes detailed information on the effects of various drugs as well as up-to-date news regarding the DEA.

"Drug Wars"

www.pbs.org/wgbh/pages/frontline/shows/drugs

> This PBS *Frontline* website chronicles the history of America's war on drugs from the 1970s to the early years of the 2000s. Visitors to the website can read interviews with drug agents, prosecutors, convicted drug dealers, and others who have been a part of the drug culture in America.

National Center on Addiction and Drug Abuse

www.centeronaddiction.org

> This website has up-to-date news on drug abuse and addiction as well as prevention and treatment.

State Medical Marijuana Laws

www.ncsl.org/research/health/state-medical-marijuana-laws.aspx

> This part of the National Conference of State Legislatures website has plenty of information on the medical uses of marijuana and a chart of each state's medical marijuana laws.

TeensHealth: Drugs and Alcohol

kidshealth.org/en/teens/drug-alcohol

> This part of the TeensHealth website contains information on different drugs and alcohol, including what each drug is and long-term effects.

INDEX

Nicole Horning has written a number of books for children. She holds a bachelor's degree in English and a master's degree in special education from D'Youville College in Buffalo, New York. She lives in Western New York with her cats and writes and reads in her free time.